YOU
A SPIRITUAL BEING

YOU
A SPIRITUAL BEING

Discover yourself and your God given
supernatural abilities and connections

Ruth Irwin

authorHOUSE®

AuthorHouse™ UK Ltd.
1663 Liberty Drive
Bloomington, IN 47403 USA
www.authorhouse.co.uk
Phone: 0800.197.4150

Published by AuthorHouse   11/23/2013

ISBN: 978-1-4918-8079-1 (sc)
ISBN: 978-1-4918-8078-4 (hc)
ISBN: 978-1-4918-8080-7 (e)

Scripture quotations taken from the Revised English Bible, copyright © Cambridge University Press and Oxford University Press 1989. All rights reserved. Word meanings taken from the 'Chambers's Twentieth Century Dictionary (1962 edition) Villafield Press, Edinburgh, Great Britain.

CONTENTS

All praise and honour to Jesus; the great 'Author' who inspired me to write this book and has been with me in every moment of my journey, in this life.

This book is dedicated to my beloved mother Mrs Clotilda Irwin and father Mr Terrance Irwin (who taught me to love God and face any challenge in life with the grace and favour of God); and to my two beautiful, loving, daughters, Esther and Joanna.

Thank you to Esther for all your love and support. You are indeed a very talented, special and kind hearted person.

Thank you to Joanna. You are my special child too and you have an incredible love for all of God's creation. God has put immense potential into you.

I have treasured every moment spent with each one of you. God bless you abundantly and grant you the desires of your heart. May the love, peace, joy and happiness of Jesus surround your lives always and keep you safe. You are God's special possessions.

"I shall win for my people praise and renown throughout the whole world." (Zephaniah 3:19 Revised English Bible).

I would like to thank my family and friends and every person who have been a part of my journey in this life, for their love and encouragement.

God's grace has always been sufficient for us.

Acknowledgements

My extremely grateful and heartfelt thanks to God, for the miracle of life itself, and for the many miracles he has performed in my life, and continues to perform. Thankfulness for loving Christian parents and each precious person who have contributed to shape my life; enriching it with so many blessings.

Thank you to my brother George and his family who have been a quiet confidence. May the Lord Jesus continue to bless you all and your ministry.

Thank you Aunt Josephine. Thank you to Maria and family.

Thank you to Miss Compton, who taught me well, encouraged, prayed and supported me in tough times.

Held close to my heart are my parents, honoured teachers and all the people who painstakingly taught me and enhanced my life with the knowledge of God. "Uncle Archie" (pastor of the Baptist Church, KGP) who was so enthusiastic and always spread the joy and love of Jesus, wherever he went.

All my wonderful school friends, the staff and students of All Saints' school made my child hood a very enjoyable happy experience; I cherish every moment, and am grateful to each one.

Thank you, to my teacher, Eleanor Nesbitt.

Acknowledgements

Thank you to all my friends along life's journey who have enhanced my life; especially Sister R.N. Paul, Mr. Solomon, Bro' G. Stephen, Jennifer, Vijaya, Raghu, Kavitha Harrison, Jane Manley, Theresa, Brian, Kay and Trevor . . .

If I haven't mentioned names of all my friends and family, you haven't been forgotten, as I do remember each one and am thankful; and grateful to God for every person.

I am a living testimony for Jesus and the glory of God.

Chapter 1

The Most Intelligent Being

Every one of us is a spirit being created in the image of God himself. Humans are the most intelligent, complex beings on the face of this earth, and yet most people are not aware that each one of us is a spirit who has a soul and lives in a body. There is however a fraction of mankind that are aware, but the majority, think that humans are just a body consisting of flesh and bones and blood, which in reality is not true. It is so important to understand one's self in this life, in order to find peace of mind, and satisfy the longing of the soul that is all the time seeking, in all the wrong places. Most people endeavour to fill the void in their lives that they don't understand or even try to understand. People willingly try to cram their lives with work or alcohol or partying or drugs to fill this unfathomable void, which is never satisfied with all this but leads only to pain and suffering that is so unnecessary. All one really needs to do, is to reconsider and unclutter one's life, of all the technology gadgets and other things that demand and hold one's attention, and spend time with yourself, to realise who you really are. It is only then that you will find out who you are, when you spend time with just yourself and God who will reveal all things to you.

The **spirit** part of a human is an immaterial **being**. This spirit person is the life of the human body. When the spirit departs, the life departs, and the human body dies, but the spirit lives on in the spirit world. The choices in life that one may make here on planet earth determines where the spirit goes when the spirit departs, after the body is shed like a change of clothes or a snakes skin, and is dead.

The **soul** of a human is the immaterial part of the spirit person that is the **intellect** or what people refer to as the sixth sense. The soul is the seat of all emotions and feelings that connect to the spirit person, which in turn connects to the flesh person, or the human body. In simple terms the soul is the brain of the spirit person just as the physical brain is a part of the flesh body. It is the satellite dish of the body, the central area of communication with higher spiritual sources.

Every person is familiar with the physical body of humans, but the spirit and soul seem non-existent, or are confusing to people. Yet they do exist, whether acknowledged or not; as they live in the human body unrecognised, until a person takes the time, to find out who they really are. This can only occur when they spend time with themselves without any of the distractions that the world has to offer.

The void that exists in every human is the longing of one's soul to be united with our Creator God, and only God can fill this void and make one complete. It is a void in the spirit person and not in the flesh person (or the body). This void exists because the Holy Spirit of God (who initially was united with the human spirit); had departed from human spirits when Adam sinned and also when we sin; but if we ask God to forgive us and ask Him into our lives again we can reconnect very easily with the Holy Spirit of God and live fulfilled, happy lives.

As humans try to fill their lives, with all that life has to offer; they are never really satisfied and never have the feeling of fulfilment. They get deeper into the desires of the flesh, thinking that these things can make them feel good. The soul or the intellect communicates the need to connect with the Creator, which goes unrecognised, as humans do not understand themselves, because they are too emotionally connected with physical things, and do not recognise the message that their own soul is sending them. A lot of people recognise the message, but then get carried away, in the spirit world, by lying, cheating deceitful spirits that exist in the spirit world, who try to counterfeit God's Spirit. This then messes up the human mind, as they connect with the supernatural counterfeit, which also exists. These are demonic spirits that are predators of the human spirit whose only aim is to capture them for eternity. There is an unseen spirit world that exists alongside our physical world, which is very real, where good and bad spirits exist. The good spirits are the angels of God and the bad spirits are the demons spirits, who are fallen angels that once were angels in heaven.

So how did humans get themselves into this situation, where they now have a void or hole in their spirits; that they try to fill up with a whole lot of things that do not give them any inner peace or satisfaction?

The Bible informs us that man was created in the image of God; and that God is a Spirit; so when Adam disobeyed God, what really happened was that his spirit got separated from his Creator, leaving a void that nothing on planet earth could fill up. Humans descended from Adam and therefore have inherited the same spiritual problem; just as anyone would inherit a disease like hypertension or diabetes that their parents or ancestors may have suffered with physically. Only the acceptance of Jesus in your life can fill this void successfully and make you feel complete, as Jesus has the Holy Spirit of God, which reconnects with our spirit and makes us complete again.

How does one accept Jesus in their spirit?

This can only be done by asking Jesus, which is verbally, speaking aloud, and asking Him to come into your life and be your Lord and Saviour.

There is a spirit world that exists, parallel to our world, whether we acknowledge it or not, it is real, and there is a heaven and a hell too; whether we acknowledge it or not; (just as real as America or any other continent or nation or planet exists, whether we believe it or not, and whether we have seen it or not). This too is a reality, when the human body dies the human spirit goes to an eternal place; and it is the choices that we have made in this life, that determine the eternal destination of our spirits, whether we acknowledge this or not and whether we have made this decision in ignorance or not.

As spirit beings in a flesh body, we live in a complex world. The Bible classifies the 'heavens' in three categories, i.e. the first heaven is the atmosphere, the stratosphere and the hemisphere of planet earth, the second heavens is the space outside the earth, and the third heavens is outside all the galaxies that we know exist, and this is where the throne room of heaven exists; where God the Father is enthroned, and Jesus is at His right hand as **King** of Kings and **Lord** of Lords. This existence of galaxies brings me back to a reasonable discussion that it is so simple and easy to believe man when he says that galaxies exist; even though we have never seen it for ourselves. Yet we find it hard to accept the facts that the Bible accounts for, that God exists and that a heaven and hell do exist. Similar to whether we believe that galaxies exist or not; the fact remains that they do, definitely, exist.

We are God's special Treasure (Exodus 19:5) **"**If only you will now listen to me and keep my covenant, then out of all peoples **you will become**

my special possession; for the whole earth is mine." Jesus compares us to the birds of the air and the flowers of the field; as to how they are clothed and fed without them having to toil or spin, and He even says that King Solomon was not arrayed like the lilies, stressing on the fact, that we are of more value to God that all of these. "Are you not worth more than the birds?" (Matthew 6:26)

God's love can be seen in everything around us, the beautiful sky every morning that he paints so differently every day. It is never the same boring sky day in and day out. It is so beautiful that artists who take so much time just to capture one moment of it on their paintings, have to painstakingly copy the exact scene on paper. Yet if we take time to notice God every morning, we will see that He cares enough to give us colour and variety in everything around us that He has created for our pleasure. Sadly, humans have found pleasure elsewhere, and got caught up in the counterfeits of the devil, and would rather watch some images on a television screen that are unreal, than spend time with a real fascinating, marvellous, God.

The need to listen to and recognise the voice of our spiritual parent as spirit beings is a dire necessity. God's voice has many facets, and the Bible refers to His voice with many different expressions, displaying the different characteristics of our loving Heavenly Father who cares about us so much. But we are so ignorant, and foolish, when we choose not to even want to know Him and all that He has to say to us, and go looking for love, in all the wrong places and get hurt in the process. Yet He is so patient with us and accepts us with all our brokenness and flaws, when we turn to Him. God's voice is very distinctly a loud voice, very well described; "his voice was like the sound of a mighty torrent." (Revelation 1:15). "I heard a sound from heaven like a mighty torrent or a great peal of thunder."(Revelation 14:2); "voice of joy"; "voice of gladness"; "voice of the bridegroom and bride"(Jeremiah 33:11); "my voice" (Psalm 81:11) The description of God's voice also portrays His magnificence, as described by the Psalmist: "The voice of the Lord in power, the voice of the Lord in majesty (Psalm 29:4)."The voice of the Lord makes flames of fire burst forth; the voice of the Lord makes the wilderness writhe in travail," (Psalm 29:7), "The voice of the Lord makes the hinds calve; He strips the forests bare," (Psalm 29:9).

The voice of the bridegroom and the voice of the bride speak about the love of God for his creation just like a bride would love her husband, and like the bridegroom would love and cherish his bride.

When we spend time with different people we begin to recognise their voices and the different tones of their voices and it does not take us long to figure out what sort of mood the person is in, just by the tone of their voice, or what emotion connects to which tone of voice. It is very similar when we spend time with God, we are able to hear His voice and recognise the tone and emotion, but if we do not spend time with Him we are not even able to hear His voice. This is why it is so crucially important to spend time with God, in His presence every day, to be able to recognise His voice and hear Him, when He guides us and gives us a word of knowledge and advice.

We do not need others to teach us how to hear His voice; in the same manner that we do not need anyone to tell us what our spouse is saying, because we spend so much of our time with our spouse and love them, that we are able to hear what they are saying, even if they do not utter any words; just their silence or body language may speak volumes to us. It is absolutely the same when we have a relationship with our Creator

God, who is our Heavenly Father, and also the Bridegroom and Bride. "The **voice of the bridegroom** and the **voice of the bride**" (Jeremiah 33:11). Rev 22:16 "**I Jesus** have sent my angel to you with this testimony for the churches . . . . Come! say the **Spirit and the bride**" and loves us so much, in so many different ways, that if we spend enough time with Him, and tarry long enough, we will be able to discern all the different facets of His voice. God communicates with our spirits, yet most times we fail to recognise His voice.

The Bible informs us that there is treasure and oil in the dwelling of the wise.

What is treasure and oil? What is the dwelling of the wise?

The dwelling of the 'wise' is our physical body, where the spirit and soul of a human dwell, or the real "me" dwells. The oil is the Holy Spirit or the "Oil of gladness" (Hebrews 1:9) as referred to in the New Testament of the Bible. The oil or the Holy Spirit lights up our spirit which is the lamp of the Lord. Jesus told the parable of the ten virgins, five of whom were wise, and five of whom were foolish; He talked about the wise virgins who had oil in their lamps (oil signifying the Holy Spirit, and the word of God) and the foolish virgins who did not have enough oil in their lamps and were not prepared when the Bridegroom (Jesus) came. This tells us what we ought to be doing to stay alert and ready for His return i.e. full of oil, in other words full of the word of God, our minds renewed with the word of God (words from the Bible which we can memorise) saturated with it and the Holy spirit; for our lamps to be burning brightly in our spirits which are 'the lamp of the Lord.' Reading and memorising as many Bible verses as we can does fill our spirit lamps, and the Holy Spirit of God will light up the lamp of our spirit.

(Acts 17:28) **"In Him we live and move in Him we exist".** When we wake up every morning, we never stop to think, how we are able to move, we take it for granted; and yet it is the Creator of the universe who has put His breath in us, and it is His power that energises our bodies to mobilise, and carry out all the necessary bodily functions that are performed every moment of our time here on earth. Even whilst we sleep and our outward body appears to be at rest; our brain and heart and all the cells in our bodies continue to work, to replenish other body cells that have worn out during our activities of the day. Without the breath of God, we could not move, we would all be dead. How much more should we acknowledge the presence of God in our lives each day and wake up with a grateful heart, that God has sustained us for yet another day to live and enjoy life and serve Him; because this is the whole duty of man i.e. 'to serve **Him.**' (Ecclesiastes 12:13) "Fear God and obey His commandments; this sums up the duty of mankind."

As complex human beings we are fully equipped with the power of God to tackle any situation that life may throw at us, and to triumphantly accomplish all our goals, that are required for a Good life that is pleasing in God's sight. (2 Peter 1:3) **"God's divine power has bestowed on us everything that makes for life and true religion."** (Acts 17:25) **"He is himself the universal giver of life and breath-indeed of everything."**

Chapter 2

"YOU", A SPIRITUAL BEING

Spirit Soul and Body,
I have given unto you,
And He dwells,
The Most High dwells in you,
All that **"I AM"**,
The all that "**I AM**",
Dwells in you,
The **power** belongs to **you,**
So keep **My commands** and live,
The Great "I AM" dwells in you.

You were created a 'masterpiece'. Revelation knowledge that the great "I AM" dwells in you is awesome. One can only begin to comprehend the meaning of this when you meditate on it. In the Bible, God refers to Himself as the '**I AM**', and declares that He dwells in us and walks in us. (2 Corinthians 6:16) "The **temple of the living God** is what **we are** . . . . I will live and move . . . . : I will be their God and they shall be my people".

When God says He is the "I AM", He is stating the fact that He is whatever you need Him to be, whatever you want, He is your "I AM" . . . . your healing, your finances, your health, your joy, your peace, whatever you desire.

Man is a **spirit;** he has a **soul,** and lives in a **body.**

The spirit person is only complete when there is a combination of the human spirit in perfect harmony with the Holy Spirit of God. This completeness can only be achieved by inviting Jesus to be the Lord of our lives, and receiving Him into our hearts, and this is when the Holy Spirit of God combines with our spirit person making us complete spirit persons. When we do not have the Holy spirit of God dwelling on the inside of us we are incomplete spirits, and this is felt physically as a void in us which seems unexplainable, as we are not familiar with the consistency of the spirit person. Our spirit without the Holy Spirit of God is a vulnerable spirit that is open to oppression, depression and possession by demonic spirits

Our soul is our human intellect in complete harmony with the Holy Spirit of God that includes the Spirit of Wisdom. Jesus has the seven Spirits of God and is this Spirit of Wisdom and also the Holy Spirit of God.

The human body is where our spirit lives and also where God's Spirit resides. We are God's temple, and this is why we should always strive to keep it holy and undefiled. "In him you also are being built with all the others into a spiritual dwelling for God." (Ephesians 2:22)

The real temple of God is a perfect combination of our spirit, soul and body, where God dwells in us, and we must keep this temple holy and clean, physically and spiritually, in our thoughts and words and actions. 1 Corinthians 3:16-17 "Surely you know that **you are God's temple, where the Spirit of God dwells**. Anyone who destroys God's temple will himself be destroyed, because the temple of God is holy; and you are that temple".

Spirit man is complete only when the human spirit and the Holy Spirit are one. 1 Corinthians 6:17 "anyone who joins himself to the Lord is one with Him spiritually".

Soul is the human intellect enhanced with God's wisdom

Human body comprises of flesh, bones and blood.

Spirit and soul and body are joined together to create God's temple.

God created humans in His image. There were two processes that took place at the beginning when God created man. He first made man a spirit being in His image, and then God made a physical body for the spirit man to live in, on this earth, out of the dust of the ground. This procedure is clearly explained in the Bible in Genesis 1:27, where it states that "God **created** human beings in His own image" (this is referring to our spirit man). Then in Genesis 2:7 we are told "The Lord God **formed** a human being from the dust of the ground and breathed into his nostrils the breath of life, so that he became a living creature." These two separate scripture recordings specifically use two different words to specify the process that God used in the making of man. The word 'created' refers to the image that God created, in His likeness, and the word formed refers to the physical flesh body.

An image is not tangible, it exists, but in the spirit world. So to make it tangible in the physical world, God had to make a physical body for this spirit that He had created. So after all the recordings of the creation of the world, God decided to give man a body, that he then **made**, out of the **dust** of the earth; and put this spirit man inside this mud body by breathing into the nostrils. 'Breathed' indicates that God articulated

His words with emphasis, and pronounced them without voice into the mud body (Adam), that he had **formed** out of the dust. So literally God's unspoken words, in the action of breathing, allowed the created spirit man; to be spoken into the body formed out of dust, making it into a 'living being'.

The **soul** is the seat of all our emotions, the part of a human that thinks feels and desires. It is the ego and the intellect of the spirit person. The soul connects to the spirit that is embodied or disembodied; the innermost being that sincerely expresses the spirit person that resides in a flesh body. The soul is the most essential part of a human, and influences the spirit which identifies with one's self, a person; the inspirer, leader, what we often refer to as our "sixth sense". A human soul is a spiritual part of the spirit man that is physically located in the belly (old English word is 'bowels') of a person. We can relate to this easily as we say 'gut feeling'. The human soul communicates with the spirit world, and is the communication centre of our whole being, as it even sends messages to our human brain in the skull. Scientific research evidence reveals that there is a "brain in our gut" which is called the Enteric Nervous system.

People in the early centuries used to make a payment to the church on behalf of a dead person as a funeral payment, for the soul, which is termed as "soul'—shot,-scot,-scat",(Chambers's Twentieth Century Dictionary (CTCD1962). This is not a Biblical principle and not what God wants us to do, but is an interesting term with a tongue twister that I have included to demonstrate that people, in days gone by, acknowledged the part of man called the 'soul'; which has lost its identity in our present generation. It is interesting, that they even thought they could make a monetary payment to the church, for the soul of a departed person. There is a minority of people in our present generation who still consider monetary payments to the church for a loved one's departed soul; believing that this can secure a place for them in heaven.

The Bible tells us, that all the souls of men belong to God, and that there is a penalty for the soul that sins, the penalty being death. All the souls that walk in God's statutes and keep His judgements faithfully are guaranteed 'life'. "Every living soul belongs to me; parent and child alike are mine. It is the person who sins that will die." (Ezekiel 18:4). "He conforms to my statutes and loyally observes my laws. Such a one is righteous: he will live, says the Lord GOD."(Ezekiel 18:9) God has also given us a free will to make decisions and choices of our own, and yet He also gives us guidance and advises us to choose life instead of death. "I offer you the choice of life or death, blessing or curse. Choose life and you and your descendents will live."(Deuteronomy 30:19).

We are **spirit**, Because God created man in His own image (God is a Spirit), we automatically become His offspring. God even refers to us as 'gods' because we are children of the Most High God. "Jesus answered, 'is it not written in your law, "I said: You are gods"? (John 10:34). "This is how love has reached its perfection among us . . . . **in this world we are as He is**." (1 John 4:17). It is amazing when we comprehend this fact, because we can begin to understand the power that has been invested in us, by God, and the potential that God has placed on the inside of each one of us. This can be compared to the fact that a mighty oak is put inside every tiny acorn. Similarly He has placed every essential ingredient that we require on the inside of us, for our journey here on this earth, for a fulfilled and prosperous life, for each one of us.

We are fully equipped; but we can only reach our full potential if we utilise all these properties that we already possess, by walking according to God's plan, and not our own. Therefore it is absolutely essential that we read our instruction manual for 'life', very carefully and follow its instructions precisely. We must listen to His voice and do as the Creator tells us to each day of our lives; to metaphorically ensure a 'glorious sunset' when it is time to depart from this life, and live eternally with God. We do have an instruction manual called the Bible, but sadly there are only a few who choose to follow the instructions for life. We all make mistakes as humans, but there is a solution to every problem, and His name is Jesus; and very simply, all that we have to do is to accept Him into our hearts, and allow Him to sit in the driving seat of our lives, to steer us back on track, and keep us on the road that leads to eternal life.

Why does the Bible specify that God **'said'**?

The word **'said'** is used in **legal language**. **'Said'** meant that it was already legally agreed upon, with the Father, Son and Holy Spirit, before God initially entered upon action; suggesting that a legal session had taken place before creation.

In the same manner when we say **'God said' we are using a 'legal language', and referring to something that God has already mentioned or named,** and by law, 'action' must happen, or be carried out, just the way action occurred when God spoke or 'said'; because the Great "**I AM**" dwells in us. The first thing that God said was "**let**" meaning: "to **allow to escape**" (CTCD 1962).

(Genesis 1:3) "God said, 'Let there be **light**" (igniting, electromagnetic radiation capable of producing visual sensation; the power of vision;

a high degree of illumination: mental or spiritual illumination; help towards understanding; knowledge; a gleam or glow in the eye or face (CTCD 1962).

When God **said 'Let'** there be **Light**; His word coming from His mouth allowed the power to escape from Him i.e. a bright source of electro-magnetic radiation, a high degree of illumination, and light came into existence.

God used the word **'let'** or spoke the word 'let' every time he created things in the first seven days, as recorded in the book of Genesis.

Light and Sound both travel and are transported from the Spiritual world, where things are unseen but exist, into a physical world where it can be seen or heard. Light gives warmth, life and strength.

Sound creates **words**, moving **substance**, and gives reaction; similar to ultra sound waves which creates lines on a graph; or for example, sound waves that can realign particles of dust and make them move according to the vibrations and frequencies.

In Genesis 1:26 the words "**let (allow to escape) US** make human beings in our image"; and Genesis 1:3 "Let there be light", indicate the word 'Let' to mean that He allowed to escape from himself an offspring with the same characteristics as himself, 'a spirit being'; when He created an image of a person. Every individual is an image; a spirit being that has wings, just like God has wings. (Psalm 91:4) "He will cover you with **His wings**".

An image is literally "formed by rays of light" that is either "refracted or reflected". The image becomes "real if the rays converge upon it" (CTCD 1962), or come closer together.

God used Light to create man in HIS image. An image always reflects light. We are made in God's image, therefore we reflect His Light that shines from His face and we also reflect His characteristics, because an image is always a reflection, or rays of light reflected. Therefore when God created us in His image He created us, as a blueprint, a masterpiece. He refers to us as 'gods' and calls us "sons of the Most High" (Psalm 82:6). In essence that the same power that raised Christ, from the dead, is living in us (Romans 8:11) "If the Spirit of Him who raised Jesus from the dead dwells in you, then the God who raised Christ Jesus from the dead will also give new life to our mortal bodies through his indwelling spirit." We have the same power as our creator God in whose **image** we are made and in whose **likeness** we are created. (Genesis 1:26) "**God said** 'Let **us** make human beings in **our image**, after our likeness". So if there was power in God's words as He spoke; therefore there is the same power in our words as we speak His words from the Bible. He has put the same power in us by creating us in His image (Our image).

Psalm 119:105 very plainly states "Your word is a lamp to my feet and a light to my path". Confirming that, **God is light.** Jesus said "I am the light of the world" (John 8:12).

Sound (**said**) by God, creates or allows to be created (**let**) light; therefore sound and light together create energy. An image (man) reflects light (God).

Because 'things' were created, after light was created, it was essential for light to be created first, as it was the main ingredient for the creation of everything else.

"Then God said 'let us make man in Our **image** according to Our **likeness**".

In (Genesis 1:27) "God **created human beings** in His own **image**; in the image of God He created him". 'Man' (spirit man) was created in God's image on the sixth day. This indicates that 'man' was first created as a **spiritual being** (the immortal or supernatural part of man) in God's image, and was later given a destructible part or a body formed out of dust, as seen in the second chapter of Genesis.

(Genesis 1:27) "Male and female He **created** them". This refers to the likeness of God, indicating that the spirit man was created in God's image in His likeness having male and female characteristics; because in this chapter God talks about the creation of man only, and that too the spirit man only, clearly referring to the creation of humans **in His image** and in **likeness to male and female**.

In (Genesis 2:7) "the Lord God **formed** a human being from the **dust** of the ground, and breathed into his nostrils the breath of life; so that he became a living creature." 'Formed' indicating a combination or the bringing together of parts which gave a shape or structure.

So the dust of the earth that God used to form a shape of a man, in combination with the breath of God, resulted in the creation of a living person. The spirit person had the Holy Spirit of God, living along side in perfect harmony with the human spirit. This combination of God's wisdom and human intellect comprises the soul of the spirit person.

The human body is just an outer shell for the spirit person that resides inside this shape of flesh, bones and blood.

The spirit man, which was created by God as an image on the sixth day, was combined with the man that was later formed of the dust. These combined together became a living image, an exact copy; an intelligent, real, human creature, made in His image, a living temple where God dwells on earth. We are His holy temple.

As recorded in the second chapter of Genesis, God specifically now "**formed** man, of the **dust** of the ground, and **breathed** into his nostrils the breath of **life;** and man became a living being." (Genesis 2:7). So this now gives the spirit man a tangible body. The spirit man, that had been earlier created, can now reside in, a dwelling place for the human spirit i.e. a flesh body. This took place when God '**breathed**' into the nostrils of this man that was formed out of the dust of the ground.

Different types of breathing have different vibrations and sounds, and signify different tones of a human voice. These can speak volumes, without even using any words; for example when a person has been jogging or has been exerting themselves, one can tell by the sounds of the persons heavy breathing; words are not required to express that there has been some exertion involved. When someone who has asthma is breathing heavily, struggling for breath and wheezing, anyone can tell that the person is in distress, it does not require spoken words to define the situation. Snoring signifies that a person is in a deep sleep. When any person is breathing with a 'death rattle', it is not difficult to recognise that the person is dying.

Different tones of breathing emphasize a specific silent language by itself, without the need of any spoken words. A sigh of contentment, a breath of delight, a sigh of relief, a sigh of sadness; can all be interpreted by any observer in silence. All these different types of breathing are types of words; pronounced without a voice. Similarly God articulated His words, **emphasised and pronounced His words without voice, by breathing** into the nostrils of this man (Adam), who had been now formed out of dust. This gave Adam the breath of life and he then became a living being. So God's **words** (**sound**) and **light** had been used to create man in His image; almost like magnetic resonance imaging that creates an image on a film (although this is an extremely inferior technology in comparison to God's super technology, which 'man' has not fathomed as yet). This spirit 'man' was pronounced by God into an earth body to become who we are; spirit soul and body.

(Genesis 2:21 and 22); "He **took** one of the man's ribs**,** and closed up the flesh over the place." "The rib he had taken out of the man the Lord God built up **into** a woman, and He brought her to the man."

So here, God now **took** or gained possession of the framework (rib) or the female characteristic out of Adam's spirit man, i.e. the likeness of God (male and female, He created them) that had been created in Adam, by God, in the beginning on the sixth day; and **made into** a woman'. In other words we are told that 'woman' arrived at her destination, or the spirit woman arrived at her destination by the movement or action of God taking her spirit out of Adam; by taking out a rib which was the route out.

In this scenario we know that God **created male and female,** and then, He **took a rib** out of Adam, and the bible says that He **'closed up the flesh in its place'**, indicating that the female characteristic of the spirit i.e. the framework—rib was taken out i.e. the female spirit component from Adam was then replaced with flesh instead of spirit.

God created the institution of matrimony in order to reunite these male and female spirit beings who were initially created as one being, because that is the original image of our Creator God.

This is why God then continues to say in (Genesis 2:24) "That is why a man leaves his father and his mother and attaches himself to his wife, and the two become one." So that the female and male components of the spirit that were created in God's likeness and were separated to create two human spirits, come together as one flesh when they are married and are not ashamed, because actually they are one, they were created as one in the Creator's image and likeness, but were separated briefly when God took the rib (or the female spirit component) out of Adam and made Eve, and then explained why a man and woman should become 'one flesh'.

The characteristic of a rib is slender and it forms a framework, it protects the thoracic cavity and its organs. Similarly a married woman forms the framework for the home, and protects her family and her husband, and is always there for them.

There are some people who are set apart by God to remain single, and are given the strength and ability by God to do so, like John the Baptist in the Bible. Any spirit beings (humans) without the Holy Spirit of God are vulnerable and are an open target for demon spirits. Yet when we possess the

Holy Spirit we are complete and become more than conquerors in Christ Jesus, and we have divine protection, provision and providence. Jesus is the greater one and He lives in us, which strengthens, empowers and gives us dominion over the power of Satan, enabling us to be in command of circumstances. The importance of keeping our spirit person and our whole body pure is a spiritual requirement by spiritual laws that govern us in this universe, even though we may be unaware of such laws.

Malachi 2:11 "The Lord's holy institution which He loves" is a husband and wife institution, or relation in matrimony which God loves, because the institution is complete and pure; similarly the prophet (Ezra 9:2) speaks of "the **Holy Seed** is mixed" when God's people pursue sexual immorality, and do not abstain from people who live immorally. The **Holy Seed** in this context is referring to God's likeness that was instilled into man at creation, i.e. 'male and female.' This is why God specifies that His temple, (who we are) should not be defiled, because when husband and wife come together the institution is complete. (1 Corinthians 7:14) "For the husband now belongs to God through his Christian wife, and the wife through her Christian husband. Otherwise your children would not belong to God, whereas in fact they do". When a third person or spirit is allowed access to a husband's or wife's body, God's temple or Holy institution is defiled, or gets contaminated with an outside spirit. God created Adam and Eve as one being when he created the spirit man in His own image.

(Malachi 2:16) "If a man divorces or puts away his wife, says the Lord God of Israel, he overwhelms her with cruelty, says the Lord of Hosts. Keep watch on your spirit and do not be unfaithful." In speaking of divorce, which has become so common in our society, God specifies very clearly, that we need to take heed i.e. take notice or pay attention and heed warnings. God straightforwardly and very simply tells us that He detests divorce. God indicates that separating a man and his wife by divorce is actually separating **God's likeness** (i.e. male and female spirits).

God hates divorce but does not hate the divorcee. We have a merciful and loving **God** who **loves each one of us**, no matter what our circumstances may be. He remembers that we are created out of dust, and overlooks all our flaws and mistakes. So just because we may have been divorced He is not angry with us, in fact he loves us and wants to heal our hurting spirits; if only we will turn to Him and ask for His divine intervention and help.

Jesus is the lover of our souls. We are able to gauge His love for us from the book of Songs of Solomon in the Bible which expresses His love for humans. (Song of Songs 6:4) "**You are as beautiful as Tirzah, my dearest**"; this tells of His divine love for each one of us. (Song of Songs 2: 9-10) "There He stands outside our wall, peering in at the windows, gazing through the lattice. My beloved spoke saying to me: "Rise up, my darling, my fair one, and come away."

God never gives up on us; He is a God that gives us second chances, as long as we are alive on this earth.

Chapter 3

Creation

As spirit beings created with splendid, unfathomable super technology by God, we are a masterpiece; and when we can fathom our intricacy it is amazing and confounding.

At the earliest stage, God (the Creator) created (brought into being) the Heavens and the earth.

Pitch black darkness! "The **Spirit of God hovered**" (Genesis 1:1). A hovering of the Holy Spirit of God! Anyone hovering surely has wings. (Psalm 91:4) "He (God) will cover you with **His wings**; you will find refuge beneath His pinions". Then a command of God; the sound of many waters as the Creator spoke and uttered words, as "God 'Said' 'Let' there be 'Light!" (Genesis 1:3) and the word coming forth from His mouth flung '**light** 'into existence; therefore **sound** from God's mouth created **light**. We know that light travels through space at a tremendous pace. There is a force, an energy, when God speaks. He doesn't shout or have to shout to create or command anything or a situation. There was surely thundering and lightening as God spoke, because the Bible states that God's voice thunders; and thunder is always preceded by lightning. It is evident that everything was created using sound waves as God spoke, said—things—were created, spoken into being—substance, came into existence created from air—sound waves. God's Word changed sound waves into 'things' that had substance and were tangible, and yet they were created by spoken words, out of the air, and came into existence. We can call the things that cannot be seen in our physical world, from the spiritual world where they exist and are waiting for us to call them out; because the Creator of the universe empowered us with the same power, in our spoken words, as our Creator, God, because He created us in His own image.

Sound (words from God) creates light that creates energy.

"In the beginning the Word already was. The Word was in God's presence, and what God was, the Word was. He was with God at the beginning, and through Him all things came to be; without Him no created thing came into being. In Him was life, and that life was the light of mankind. The light shines in the darkness, and the darkness has never mastered it" (John 1:1-5).

Jesus is the Word and was present at the creation of the world as the 'Word'; the Holy spirit of God was present as the 'Spirit of God' (Genesis 1:2) hovering, and God the Father was present as well creating things by speaking and declaring them.

Jesus was the spoken 'Word' that was spoken by God; living words that created everything when spoken. Father God was speaking, Jesus was the living Word being spoken and the Holy Spirit of God gave life to living things. (John 6:63) "It is the Spirit (Holy Spirit) that gives life . . . . the Words (Jesus) I (God) have spoken to you are both spirit and life". A prior agreement had been made at a legal session in heaven before the creation of the world as indicated by the word 'said'; which is legal terminology. God knew us long before we were born, because he predestined us. "For those whom God knew before ever they were, He also ordained to share the likeness of His Son" (Romans 8:29)

God initially created light, as that was the basic ingredient required for everything that followed. God the Father spoke light into being when "God said **'let' (allow to escape)** there be **light**" (Genesis 1:3). The light that was allowed to escape from His face came into existence when He said 'let'. It caused bright illumination; it was light which has laser, electro-magnetic and radio frequency characteristics. This bright light needed to be contained, in spheres having boundary lines that could not be crossed without the Father's command. God permitted light to escape from His face in a limited large amount when He spoke. Light is the basic unit of data, required for any task and for the growth and functioning of all of God's creations.

Light is also defined as a "conspicuous person" (CTCD 1962). No one else other than Jesus could be this conspicuous person. (John 8:12) "Jesus . . . . I am the light of the world". The only person that can emit light in such a terrific manner is God.

Illuminating light which God allowed to escape from Himself in large controlled amounts was separated into two different shades as God divided the light from the darkness and called it 'day and night.'

Because we are spirits who live in a flesh body, it would be easy for our bodies to be consumed by fire with this kind of heat and high degree radiation light. Therefore God in all His goodness and love for us created lights in the heavens to contain this heat and illumination which would also help mankind as markers for events, times and seasons (Genesis 1:14) "God said, **'Let (allow to escape)** there be **lights** in the vaults of heaven to separate day from night, and let them serve as signs both for festivals and for seasons and years." After God allowed the amount and kind of light to escape from his face that He required for these great

25

lights in the heaven, He then made the kind of lights that he desired. (Genesis 1:16) God **made** two great **lights**, the greater to govern the day and the lesser to govern the night; He also **made** the **stars."**

God **made** celestial bodies (spheres, containers) for this created light i.e. the sun and the moon and determined their boundaries; so as not to incinerate His creation, and yet provide them with warmth and light that is so essential for life.

We are made aware of where this high degree illuminating light was emitted from, by the apostle John in the book of Revelation in the Bible where a description of Jesus is given, as John was permitted to see in the vision (Revelation 1:14) **"His eyes flamed like fire."** This illustrates that the light that God allowed to escape from His face was emitted from His eyes at creation, and He then made celestial bodies (sun, moon and stars) or containers for this bright light to be contained and have boundaries.

When Christ returns to the earth, our flesh bodies will be transformed. The new city of Jerusalem will not have a sun and a moon and stars, to illuminate it because God's light will be sufficient, and will not consume us then because our flesh bodies will be non-existent as they will have been transformed; so the light will not affect our spirit bodies (Revelation 21:23) "The **city did not need the sun or the moon** to shine on it, for the glory of God gave it **light**, and it's lamp was the **Lamb**" (Jesus is known in the Bible as "the Lamb who was slain for us"). This new city will not need the sun or moon because there will be no danger of the light of God burning up our disembodied spirits which will have been transformed.

Here on earth there is a danger of us being consumed by fire or this high powered light because we are living in a body that consist of flesh, which is corruptible and can be ignited. Hence the need here on earth for celestial bodies i.e. sun, moon and stars to contain the heat of the electro-magnetic light, and to prevent the flesh part of humans from being consumed by fire.

Can you imagine what would have happened if God had not created the sun and the moon?

The direct bright source of high degree illuminating, or igniting light, emanating from His face would incinerate, or ignite us all and the whole world; so instead He made the sun and allowed the sun to be ignited with the light shining forth, from his face. So when you see the sun, every morning, what you are really seeing, is the light shining from God's face, being reflected from the sun so that it does not ignite us. It is impossible to even comprehend how much light, God really is, or the magnificence or splendour of His complete form, that is light, as it is only a small portion of light shining from his face only or allowed to shine from His face as agreed upon (**said**) is **let** or allowed to ignite the sun.

The Father, the Son, and the Holy Spirit are one God; and they have seven spiritual attributes which are the seven Spirits of God. (Revelation 3:1) "These are the words of the one who has the seven spirits of God and the seven stars". The Spirit of Wisdom is referred to as 'She', who is also one of the seven spirits of God, being the female component of God. The Holy Spirit, always referred to as 'He' being the male component.

At creation (Genesis 1:26) when "God said 'let Us make human beings in our image, after our likeness", He permitted an image of 'US' (Father, Son, Holy Spirit and seven Spirits of God) to escape from Himself in light form (a spirit being) that came into existence as 'man'. Thus a spirit 'man' was created in His image, according to His likeness. All the characteristics of God were present in our spirit 'man'; because God allowed a replica of Himself; a blue print to escape from Himself when He spoke Words. A powerful highly sophisticated technology was used by God at creation which is beyond our comprehension. To understand the concept we can only liken the similarity to Magnetic Resonance Imaging which is a human technology that is extremely inferior in comparison.

God created our spirit 'man' and blessed 'man' (spirit 'man') and commanded 'man' to fill the earth and increase and multiply, and have dominion over everything on the earth. Our spirit was created with all the components and characteristics of God and is powered supernaturally as we are connected directly to God by invisible light rays, as we draw all that we need from God. Our Father God is the beacon light in the throne room of heaven.

The born again spirit 'man' has the spiritual DNA of God. To be 'born again' means to re-connect with the Holy Spirit of God, by asking Jesus to be the Lord of our lives. The blood of Jesus which He shed at Calvary is able to cleanse us on a daily basis. (1John 1:7) "If we live in the light as He himself is in the light, then we share a common life, and the blood of Jesus cleanses us from all sin". Only a born again spirit person is able to have the 'mind of Christ' but this is freely available to all and depends on the choice that we make. The mind of Christ is essential as it instructs us in our daily lives and gives us inside information; enhancing our lives as we are able to have a varying perspective on any situation. (1Corinthians 2:16) "We possess the mind of Christ".

We are made in God's image therefore we reflect His light and characteristics, because an image is always a reflection. God is light (Psalm 119:105) "Your word is a lamp to my feet and a light on my path."

We were spoken into being as images, a perfect replica of our Creator God as He allowed His form and likeness to escape from Himself into this intricately created spirit person, known as human beings. To create this image (spirit person) "God said 'Let' **(allow to escape) US**, make human beings in Our image, after Our likeness, to have dominion over the fish in the sea, the birds of the air, the cattle, all wild animals on land and everything that creeps on the earth."(Genesis 1:26). "God created human beings in His own image; in the image of God He created them; male and female He created them."(Genesis 1:27). This spirit human being was created as a female and male personality as the likeness of God (who has male and female components) escaped from God to form 'man', who now had a dual sexuality, before these spirit persons were separated into separate flesh bodies that God made out of mud first for Adam, and then took Eve's spirit (female) spirit out of Adam when He took a rib out of Adam and made it into a woman. This concept of the male and female components being together, in one spirit is not difficult to understand when we compare the similarity with flowers, that have the male and female components in the one flower together, i.e. the stamens (female) and the pistol (male) of the flower. The Holy Spirit is referred to in the Bible as 'He', and the Spirit of Wisdom as 'She'; confirming both the male and female characteristics of God.

God made you and me 'creators'. God is the Creator, and having **His likeness**, would make us perfect replicas, giving us the same **power**, as our **Creator**, in whose **'image'** we are made, and in whose **'likeness'** we are created. When we accept Jesus into our hearts this power is activated again, which was temporarily lost when Adam and Eve sinned. The same power that raised Jesus from the dead is living in us; therefore He who raised Christ from the dead will also give life to our mortal bodies through His Spirit who now dwells in us.

If there was **power** in **God's words** as He spoke; this definitely implies that there is the same power in our words, as we speak; **His words** from the Bible; because He has invested the same power in us by creating us in **His image**; or as it is written **'Our image'** (notice the **'Our'**: meaning that God is referring to a plural form, which includes the **Father**, **Son** and the **Holy Spirit'**).

God's light is a power supply that we can connect with in our spirits as we communicate with Him. God knows that our human capacity is limited as the physical body is destructible, and therefore controls the light supply in our bodies, and in the universe.

Have we ever questioned the existence of electric currents that run through our body every day, and ever wondered what their source is or where their origin is from and what keeps it going?

'Man' is fully aware that the heart and brain have electrical impulses that can be monitored by carrying out tests such as an Electro-cardiogram, or an Electro-encephalogram; these impulses are measured by these tests. But what causes these electrical impulses? It is God's light in you.

When we confess God's words they are similar to a high voltage current that burns out impurities, just like laser technology, that is used, for example, to blast kidney stones or bladder stones; Confessing is speaking God's words; scriptures from the Bible that are relevant to your situation in life, that is required to bring about positive outcomes. God's words when spoken, allows God's light to flood our entire being. God's 'Word' and the Holy Spirit is the 'power switch' that we as believers have access to; power that is available to us, in the spoken word of God. It is up to each one of us to use this God given ability of speech, to speak His words, every day of our lives to enable us to live victoriously; and utilise the huge power supply that has been invested in us which stems from our Creator. It is a source that will never run out. It is the light of God that purifies our lives spiritually and physically.

"I shall make my words a fire in your mouth," (Jeremiah 5:14).

There are two spiritual persons that God refers to, and they are the 'Holy Spirit' (He); and Wisdom (She), who enrich our spiritual lives, intervening divinely, and guide us in everything we do. The scriptures tell us that we are sealed with the Holy Spirit, when we accept Jesus in our hearts and are saved by grace. The Holy Spirit is a gift from God freely given to us at Salvation. The Bible mentions that wisdom has to be acquired; even though we are created complete in the likeness of God. Adam sinned and he lost 'Wisdom' or the 'likenesses of God, when he disobeyed God, and since we are all descendents of Adam, it is up to each one of us to obtain this 'Wisdom' from God, which was initially part of the package deal that Adam lost, but is still available to us if we will seek God and ask Him. This Spirit of Wisdom is also Jesus, who is also light.

How did Adam lose Wisdom?

It could be logically explained, that Adam and Eve lost wisdom from their eyes, when they sinned against God; because they were told not to let wisdom **depart** from their **eyes,** but they were to keep wisdom (Proverbs 3:21) "My son . . . do not let them out of your sight." This verse is an indication that Adam and Eve possessed the spirit of Wisdom; as this is the likeness of GOD, but they let Wisdom depart from their eyes, when Eve **saw** that the tree was good for food, and it was pleasant to the **eyes**. (Genesis 3: 6) informs us that "she ate, —and he ate, then the **eyes** of both of them were **opened.**"

Only when a container is opened, can its contents be spilled out or depart from it; so **two** corresponding **actions** are to be observed here, that occurred in this context:

Saw= opened eyes,

Ate= opened mouth,

Adam and Eve both sinned by eating the forbidden fruit with their mouths; and therefore by putting into their mouth (or opening their container or vessel) what should not have been put in, Wisdom was pushed out. This action caused what was originally inside, i.e. Wisdom, to get pushed out; or depart from their eyes; because they were now focusing on visions of things, that God had forbidden them to touch or **eat**; so their vessels or spirits were defiled, or left devoid of Wisdom. This departing of Wisdom from the human spirit created a yearning, which nothing else can fulfil. Therefore without the 'She' component or the 'likeness' of God—a human is incomplete and restless, because a void, was created when Wisdom departed.

Eyes are the light of the body, therefore spiritual light can shine through or emanate from the eyes of one's body, if **Jesus** the "**light of life**" (John 8:12), is living in you. But if a person sins and allows **sin** (demon spirit) and **darkness** to enter into their bodies, then light can only exit from the eyes, and as a consequence that person is left in complete darkness inside, and this explains why people who sin, are unable to comprehend the things of God; because Wisdom-Jesus-Light has departed from their eyes, leaving them in utter darkness inside themselves. But when Jesus is received by confession, the mouth being the opening to our spiritual container, or vessel, Jesus fills our vessels (lamp), and spiritual light is then emitted from us through our eyes, for all to see.

The light of God is a vital ingredient for Salvation; (Isaiah 49:6) specifically mentions "I shall appoint you a **light** to the nations, so that my salvation may reach earth's farthest bounds." This is evident in our present world, where literally light beams are used to transfer God's healing power by images of God's people and sounds all around the world, by television and other media, through His ministers on earth who have been anointed for a healing ministry.

(Isaiah 42:6) "I have formed you and destined you to be a **light** for peoples, a **lamp** for nations".

"The Lord shines into a person's soul, searching out his innermost being."(Proverbs 20:27) Our spirit, when united with God's Spirit, burns brightly, and shines in the spiritual darkness of this world; it is visible in the spirit world as God's candle. The demon spirits and the angels can see it clearly; and we are a threat to demon spirits who can see our spirit candles burning brightly with the oil of the Holy Spirit of God.

We are all aware that both light and sound travel through space transported from the spiritual world on Radio Frequency waves (RF) that are unseen but yet exist, to the physical world where it can be seen and heard. Light and Sound both travel, and have frequencies that can be measured.

Light gives warmth, life and strength and has physical and spiritual properties that merge.

Sound creates words, moves substance and gives reactions similar to ultra sound, which creates lines on a graph and patterns on sounding depth. Vibrations can realign particles depending on the force of the vibrations, just as the sound of words can realign things in our present and future spiritually, which then manifest in the physical realm. The words we speak are powerful they shape our future.

Jesus is the light of the world; He is very literally the physical and spiritual light, and is in control of the entire universe. Light is powerful laser beams; energy that burns. The light of Jesus (spiritual and physical) produces healing from the inside to the outside of the body (God's temple). In our world today, light beams are literally being used to transport the spiritual light of Jesus to the nations, using satellite beams and television and other media. The spiritual light of God literally merges with the physical light that is visible in the world.

God used Light in a more highly sophisticated technique that is similar to the principle of Magnetic Resonance Imaging, plus Sound (Words) to create man in His own image. This is much more acceptable to believe when we understand the scientific principles that God used, when He spoke man into being, or when he created man, i.e. a spirit being first, before he made a human body for man out of the dust of the ground, as described in the second chapter of the book of Genesis.

His Words are more powerful than an MRI machine that creates an image. God's words give the image tangible substance, as the spirit man is put into a human body made with mud.

Magnetic Resonance Imaging uses Radio Frequency waves to generate images of the human body in our world of technology, and it is known that if the human body comes in contact with high power frequency currents, it can cause serious RF burns.

(Exodus 33:20) "My face you cannot see, for no mortal may see me and live . . . . I shall put you in a crevice of the rock and cover you with my hand until I have passed by . . . . My face must not be seen". This explains why God covered Moses with His Hand and hid him in the cleft of the rock when He was passing by, and Moses was not permitted to look upon the face of God; to avoid Moses from getting incinerated, as **God is light**. The light emanating from God's face could have ignited Moses and burned him to a cinder, in a flash. 1 Timothy 6:16 explains God "He alone possesses immortality, dwelling in unapproachable light; Him no one has ever seen or can see". It is very clear that God dwells in unapproachable light.

Chapter 4

Spirit Man

The spirit man can feel, **taste, touch, smell and hear**; and this is clearly depicted in the parable that Jesus told about the rich man and Lazarus. After the rich man and Lazarus both died; the rich man could **see** Lazarus, in Abrahams bosom, and he **spoke** to Abraham from hell, asking him to allow Lazarus to dip his finger in water and **touch** his tongue, to reduce the heat in his body, which he could **feel**, and he could **hear** Abraham reply to him.

To hear the voice of God we have to fine tune our spirits, to the same radio frequencies of God by living a life in the Spirit, according to His word. The natural man cannot hear the voice of God because it requires spiritual discernment, the spiritual radio frequencies need adjustment, and to align these fields requires some action on our part. Our spirit man, needs the anointing of God first, upon our life or vessel, and only then can our vessels be filled with the Wisdom of God; and can be taught; and this process can only take place when we accept Jesus into our hearts and lives, allowing the Holy spirit of God to gain access to our spirit man, and make the necessary adjustments.

When we confess the Word of God (words from the Bible) daily, and speak it with our mouth, God's Spirit is then enabled to make all the mathematical adjustments and fine tune the frequencies of our spirits, to the things of God and have a perfect alignment with Him. The more we spend time in the word of God, confessing it with our mouths, the more tuning takes place in our spirit till finally we are able to discern in our spirits, what the Lord is saying to us in life's situations. Just like a baby that is helpless at birth, and does not know how to communicate, but has to listen and learn from his parents first, before he actually begins to speak; similarly we have to listen to the words of our Heavenly Father and learn before we can communicate, with our Heavenly Father, God, and recognise His voice. Just as babies learn to recognise the voices of their parents and voices of others, and know who are, his /her, own kin, we must learn too. We are so often told in the Bible "You have ears, so hear what the Spirit says to the churches!" (Revelation 2:29). God is telling us to listen, to be able to hear, and in order to be able to listen spiritually we are given specific instructions, to receive God's words in our hearts, so as to enable our spiritual hearing.

(Ezekiel 3:10) "Listen carefully, O man, to all that I have to say to you, and **take it to heart.**" When we learn and master this super powered communication system, and are able to use this high technology 'direct communication line' available to us, the prophet Isaiah informs us in (Isaiah 30:21) "If you stray from the path, whether to right or to left, you will hear a voice from behind you sounding in your ears saying 'This is the way follow it."

We are created an absolute marvel, in the image of God, by our Creator God, and we can only comprehend it partially, because the intricacy of the human body is still being discovered. Medical science research evidence informs us that we have a Central Nervous System which is controlled by the brain in our skull, and also an Enteric Nervous System controlled by the brain in our gut.

So why would the human body need two brains?

What is the spiritual purpose of this highly complex brain in the gut that spans the entire alimentary canal, from the oesophagus to the bowels (belly)?

The physical Enteric Nervous system is the physical location of the soul of the spirit man which is also the communication centre with the spiritual realm. To believers, this is not an enigma, because the Bible clarifies this "He that believeth on me, as the scripture hath said, **out of his belly** shall flow rivers of living water," (John 7:38). The 'belly' as we are all familiar with, is the part of the human body that is below the ribs which also contains the stomach and the bowels. We all know that our "belly" is the seat of our emotions, because whenever we feel any sort of emotion it immediately affects our stomach and we feel a fluttering sensation in our tummies, or our throats seem to be caught up when we get emotional and we have a problem communicating, at this stage, and feel a lump in our throats.

So why would our "gut" also have a second brain?

From a Biblical perspective it is very clear that this is the central area of communication for the spirit of humans, and that explains why we have a 'gut feeling', when decisions are to be made, and we put it down to a sixth sense, but really; it is the Spirit of God communicating with us; helping us to make a right decision or trying to give us an instruction. But we are unable to decipher the sound of, or recognise the voice of God, because we have not spent enough time in His presence, listening to His voice, to be able to decipher the sounds. The prophet Jeremiah was tuned into the Spirit of God and recognised the voice of God, because his spiritual ears were tuned into the frequencies of God; his soul could hear in his spirit, his inner most being which he described as his bowels he says "(Jeremiah 4:19) "Oh how I writhe in anguish, how my heart throbs! I cannot keep silence, for I hear the sound of the trumpet, the clamour of the battle cry."

In the book of Revelation (Bible) the voice of the Lord is described as the sound of trumpets. Jeremiah knew that the brain of his spirit man i.e. his "soul" was in his bowels (belly), because his spirit man was able to hear, the voice of God, in his bowels (belly). This scripture clearly explains in human terms, why the human body has two brains that work independent of each other, because the brain of the physical body is in the head or skull, and controls the flesh body, but the brain of the spirit man is in the gut of man which is the soul of the man and has a memory of all the experiences in life that we face, which are remembered, when the spirit leaves the body after death; as depicted, in the story of the rich man and Lazarus the beggar.

We see that the rich man has a memory and can remember his past life, because he talks about his brothers who are still alive on the earth. Biblical instances suggest that our emotions are influenced by the soul, and emotional well being relies on the messages sent from the gut brain to the brain in the skull. So literally the brain in the gut tells the brain in the head what to do. What the Bible says now makes sense "Dear friend, above all I pray that things go well with you, and that you may enjoy good health: I know it is well with your soul."(3 John 1:2).God refers to us as his beloved, and implies that when our soul is in good health it influences the health of our physical body.

The renewing of your minds is the important process so that the brain in our gut (soul) is then able to send healing command signals to the brain in our skulls; which in return send command signals to every cell in our body, re-setting them all to healing mode. We must confess God's words with our mouths first in order to renew our thinking process to enhance good health. It is well with my soul! And I pray that all who read this book will be able to say with me "It is well with my soul."AMEN.

Chapter 5

The Power Source for Humans

"In HIM we live, and move, in Him we exist," (Acts17:28). Every human being on planet earth is individually connected, and wired up, to the Most High God of the universe, whether we know it or not and whether we acknowledge it or not. We are wired up, connected to the Most High God in the most intricate manner that man can ever comprehend. God's heart beats in man, who is so intricately designed and created by God. We are created wonderfully (Psalm 139:14) "wonderful you are and wonderful your works."

Many of us are aware that our body functions on electrical current as every cell in our body is electrically charged, and these currents are measured on graphs when we go for an investigation i.e. electro-cardiogram (ECG) or electro-encephalograms (EEG). Have we ever stopped to question where the mains are; or what is our power source? In our physical world we know that cars have engines, and need to have fuel in the engines for the cars to run smoothly. Similarly electrical items, for example televisions are no good if they are not connected to a power source and switched on. So what is this power source that makes our bodies work on a daily basis? Even when we are asleep, our brains still give out electrical signals that can be measured and our hearts still beat within us non-stop.

In the Bible the Lord mentions "I AM the ALPHA and the OMEGA', says the Lord God, who is, who was, and who is to come, the sovereign Lord of all" (Revelation 1:8). God is telling us literally that He is the

'Alpha' or the power source by which humans function, even though a lot of people may not acknowledge the fact.

The word 'Alpha' clearly speaks for itself, and reveals to every Christian and all who believe in the Lord Jesus Christ, the true meaning of what Jesus is trying to tell us. "In HIM we live and move and have our being"; literally specifying that we are connected directly to God the Father who is the 'Father of **lights**'. Our power source is from heaven, from God Himself, the Alpha; being the electrical power source in our brains, and the chains of haemoglobin in our blood and the emitter, the electrical waves that connect us or wire us up to God.

Yes, every cell in the human body communicates via electrical impulses and are held together by the power of our Creator God the 'ALPHA!'; the scaffolding of every cell that connect all tissue in the human body. (Colossians 1:17) "All things are held together in Him" All electrical impulses in our bodies work in circuits which are complex mathematical calculations. There is human medical research evidence of mathematical and chemical communication in cells of our bodies.

When we remain connected to God and walk in his ways i.e. in the way that He planned for us and designed for us, we remain in divine health, especially when we confess the word of God daily, as this process allows the realignment of the structure of the body cells and changes the mathematical calculations in our bodies to remain in 'healing mode' or 'health mode. The sounds of God's words change the molecular structure of cells in our body. The sounds of different words, thoughts and sounds of music make different wave patterns on graphs. It is amazing; and it gives us an insight into why God instructs us to confess the words of God, because it changes the patterns in our cells (which have an electrical charge), mathematically and physically, and these words, create electrical circuits and make beautifully intricate patterns.

When we do things that we want to do that are out of God's will for us, we somehow break the electrical connections and circuits, and the power source gets restricted or cut off, causing the human body to malfunction. These malfunctions occur when we go against the spiritual laws of God, and there is a diversion from the power source. To rectify any malfunction, the practical answer is to connect back to the mains, and this can be done by accepting Jesus into our hearts as our personal Lord and Saviour by asking Him to be the Lord of our lives. The Bible informs us that when we accept Jesus in our hearts, we are translated from the kingdom of darkness into the kingdom of light. For a light to shine a switch must be turned on, that connects to a power supply.

God in the Old testament Bible refers to Himself as the '**I AM**', and Jesus in the book of Revelation, in the New Testament, also refers to Himself as the '**I AM**' the Alpha and Omega. God is a 'Master of Arts' as he paints the sky differently every moment of the day. God (I AM) is also an 'assembly member of the FATHER, SON, and the HOLY SPIRIT. 'I AM' is God, the broadcaster from heaven, **broadcasting, audio signals, just as on earth we use amplitude modulation,** as a means of **broadcasting.**

'I AM' is the Spiritual DNA of the Most High God that is in each one of us, these are molecules that encode our spiritual genetics as well as our physical genetics. God is in absolute control of the entire universe. He is the Power source, of the Sun and the Moon and of every living thing that moves upon this planet and solar system.

He truly is an awesome God. Without God there would be no life at all. The complexity of His super technology is incomprehensible to the human understanding, but the simplicity of it all is that we do not have to understand or comprehend to believe, in order to receive from Him. All we have to do is to love Him and trust Him with childlike faith, and He will work everything for our good. "And in everything as we know, he co-operates for good with those who love God and are called according to his purpose" (Romans 8:28)

Chapter 6

HIM=His Imperial Majesty

Power

All through the Bible there is this simple word "HIM", yet many have never stopped to think of the meaning and the simplicity of this word. In this word is hidden so much power and energy that comes from the person, who this word refers to. The Great 'I AM,' the 'Alpha and the Omega', and the 'Him' that the Word of God constantly refers to; His Majesty on High, the King of all the earth, His Imperial Majesty Jesus who gave his life for us, so that we might have eternal life. We underestimate the power that is invested in us, and the authority that we have. We have the power of the Kingdom of Heaven backing us up, when we speak or move anywhere; the power of His Imperial Majesty.

As spirit beings created in the exact image of God Himself; "God is a Spirit" (John 4:24) we are directly connected to the throne room of heaven, and have in us, all the capabilities and radio frequency waves in us of light, sound and energy that we can ever fathom, but many of us still crawl around as helpless little creatures, only because we choose to be ignorant. Every cell in our body communicates with each other throughout the day and night, using this super powered technology; sending messages to our brain and other parts of our bodies. Yet we seem to be so unaware of all the activity that goes on, inside of us each day, whether we are waking or whether we are sleeping. The kinetics and dynamics, of our bodies continue nonstop.

An illustration of a particular scenario during the life of Jesus, here on earth as described in the Bible depicts a vivid scene in (Luke 6:19) "and everyone in the crowd was trying to touch Him, because power went out from Him and cured them all". The people of Jesus' time knew that Jesus had some super natural powers that were transferrable, and in their simplicity they were reaching out to touch Him, so as to transfer this power surge into their bodies for the restoration of their health. This power came from the spiritual Light which cleans out or burns out impurities, and dross, like laser beams; bringing healing to body, mind and spirit; and these people recognised this.

Power is energy. Supernatural beings, deity, have power or force. A person or organisation that is strong has power. Power is the authority given or delegated to a person or body, and also indicates the military strength of the kingdom. Power gives one the capacity or ability to carry out a task in a specific manner. Power empowers an individual's speech, and powers of concentration and also enables them to influence the behaviour of others or the course of events, as it is backed up by authority and authorizes rights meted out to persons who are citizens of that particular kingdom. Power has a mathematical calculation, and a specific circuit; and Jesus has this super power.

Luke 8:46 "Jesus said, somebody did touch me, for I felt that power had gone out from me."

Mark 5:30 "Aware at once that power had gone out of Him, Jesus turned around in the crowd and asked 'Who touched my clothes?"

Jesus knew that He had the power in Him; which was a supply of spiritual energy that transferred, and travelled with great speed; even though He was in a temporary human body here on earth. It was even transferable as it travelled at such great speed to the woman in the story as she had just touched his clothes; because Jesus immediately became aware of this power leaving His body, and being transmitted to the woman through His clothes. This super high voltage spiritual power from His Imperial Majesty, travelling at such a high speed and frequency passed through the clothing of Jesus to the woman, healing her completely and instantaneously. Jesus felt the impact, even though He was in a crowd because of the power surge that left His Body, at the faith of the woman's words and actions of touch, i.e. faith in action, was tangible.

We are all aware that clothes which come in contact with the human body acquire a static current, and this can be felt when we put our clothes on or take them off, proving in a very simple manner that our human bodies are conductors of electricity. Be reassured, that this super power lies dormant in each of us, as we are already connected or wired up to His Imperial Majesty, and only have to draw from Him, in faith, by confessing the Word of God, and combining it with the corresponding actions required, to set our faith in motion. This flicks on the spiritual power switch instantly, allowing a spiritual power surge in our direction, to carry out the desired task or healing that may be necessary.

The woman who touched Jesus for her healing had spoken out first in faith, and then her corresponding action of faith was to touch the garment of Jesus. The fact that Jesus is majestic and magnificent and comes to us from the empire of God in all His glory, who reveals His power literally and metaphorically, because we know Him as the King of Kings and Lord of Lords, and it is He who is the One in complete command of the universe, and is the highest authority. We can comprehend with our human thinking the enormity of His saving power, healing power, and providing power that transports all that we need instantly, so simply from the spirit world into our physical world, by the power of His name, and the spoken word of God. We can enjoy all that he has in store for us, and live the abundant life that He desires for us to live. The promise of eternal life is only granted to those who will repent and accept Jesus as Lord and Saviour.

"Dear friend, above all I pray that things go well with you, and that you may enjoy good health: I know it is well with your soul." (3 John 1:2) We are super powered and fully equipped, by our Creator God. "Remember the Lord your God; it is He who gives you strength to become prosperous," (Deuteronomy 8:18). He gives strength to the weary, and he also increases our strength.

Chapter 7

Spiritual Laws that Govern Spirit Beings on the Earth

Whether we acknowledge it or not; there are spiritual laws that govern and affect every human being on planet earth. Almost every individual is unaware of the existence of a spiritual world that exists alongside our physical world, and most people will even scoff at the person who tries to convince them that this is true. Like it or not, believe it or not, ignore it or not; it is very real and it even controls our destinies if we are not careful. When God created man He gave man a 'free will', and it is this same will; that enables us to make the right or wrong choices, about which kingdom we choose to be governed by, and consequently which kingdom laws should govern us. God in all His love for mankind has allowed us to choose, and if we don't choose at all, then the devil has the authority to govern us under his legal system which also exists.

It is very clearly mentioned in the Bible, that the devil has principalities and powers. We are made aware that there definitely are two kingdoms in the spiritual realm, i.e. God's kingdom (God's legal system), in which Jesus is our advocate, and makes life absolutely easy for us, if we will only believe on Him, and accept Him, into our hearts. There is also a demonic kingdom that is governed by Satan. These two kingdoms have two different laws that are in motion:

- The Law of the Spirit of life in Christ Jesus.
- The law of sin and death.

It is essential to take note of the fact that a kingdom always has a king and minister as the highest authority. In the case of the 'Law of the Spirit of life in Christ Jesus' the spiritual ruler of this Kingdom is Jesus as this is God's Kingdom.

In the case of the 'law of sin and death' the spiritual leader is a demon spirit named 'sin', and his accomplice named 'death', who is also a demon spirit.

The Law of the Spirit of Life in Christ Jesus

"In **Christ Jesus** the life giving law of the Spirit has **set you free from** the law of **sin and death**" (Rom 8:2). This scripture makes it absolutely apparent and crystal clear that we are set free from these demon spirits named 'sin' and 'death'; under God's law in His Kingdom.

This law has multiple benefits and enables us to live our lives to the fullest, trusting in the Lord for our every need and desire. We are governed by this Kingdom law and we allow this law to govern our lives, when we make the choice to accept Jesus as our Lord and Saviour. The Bible specifies that we are translated from the kingdom of darkness into the Kingdom of Light (Kingdom of God). Our families and our children are also protected by this spiritual law when we make this choice.

The law of the Spirit of life in Christ Jesus makes us 'spiritually minded' and gives us life and peace. It causes us, not to be debtors to the flesh, or to the desires of the flesh, because by the Holy Spirit's power the deeds of our body that cause us to sin are put to death. Therefore we do not even have to struggle with various desires, to fulfil the lust of the flesh, because the Holy Spirit causes us to make the right choices and gives us the strength and courage to do so. Therefore the deeds of the body are put to death, causing us to live. Those who are led by the Spirit of God are sons of God.

This Law of the Holy Spirit gives our mortal bodies life. When walking according to the Spirit; there is no condemnation to those who are in Christ Jesus, and the 'Spirit of life', makes intercession for the saints, according to God's will, with groaning. It searches our hearts, and enables us to eagerly wait in hope with perseverance. The Spirit of life gives us all things, freely. We are justified and God's elect cannot legally be charged, because Jesus makes intercession for us and has paid the price, in full, for us, with His Blood.

This law ensures that we are not separated from the love of Christ, and also ensures that through famine, persecution, nakedness, peril and wars, we are more than conquerors. Children of the Spirit of life, most importantly, are the "seed of God".

This law of God is served with the mind, and this is why we are specifically instructed, to renew our minds with the Word of God, so as to be able to serve God according to the Law of God's kingdom, so as to exercise our Kingdom rights.

The Law of Sin and Death

Romans 8:2 "In Christ Jesus the life giving law of the Spirit has set you free from **the law of sin and death**"

This is the legal system that also operates on planet earth, in the spiritual realm, and is governed by demon spirits, two of which are named one is 'sin' and the other is 'death'. These are fallen angels who rebelled against God and were thrown out of heaven. Both these are spirit beings, but are demon spirit beings, belonging to a demonic kingdom, that is a counterfeit, of the Kingdom of God. This demonic kingdom also has principalities and powers, that are counterfeit, and the Bible warns us that "Satan" masquerades as an "angel of light" (2 Corinthians 11:14), and can also perform signs and wonders. We are warned not to be fooled or tricked by these demon spirits, but are instructed and told to discern the spirits, to know who they are.

This law of sin is served with the flesh by fulfilling the desires and lust of the flesh, and children of the flesh are not the seed of God.

This law of sin and death operates in the minds of people; and to be carnally minded is a trait of this law, which leads to death, that is physical as well as spiritual. If a person is carnally minded he/she cannot please God but is enmity, against God.

The law of sin and death is not subject to the law of God, and cannot be subject to the law of God. It causes people to be 'debtors '. It causes people to live according to the desires of the flesh, or the sensual desires of the flesh, causing them to be slaves to 'sin' (demon spirit) and 'death' (demon spirit). By being subject to this law the mindset of people becomes set or ingrained with this way of life which appears perfectly normal to them, because they are spiritually blinded. Like a computer, what they have fed into their minds now begins to direct their way of life, and they serve this law of sin and death with the flesh by fulfilling the lusts of the flesh, and are caught in a vicious circle; that only leads to spiritual death and destruction of the spirit man and the physical man.

Being a slave to sin also brings or allows sickness to reign in their bodies and minds, and spirits; causing a bondage and slavery to these demons spirits, who play havoc in the lives of people, only because they are ignorant of the fact that this demonic hierarchy exists. They are totally unaware, and therefore they haven't made a choice, and come automatically under the reign of this demonic kingdom. It is dangerous, but absolutely true, and therefore we need to "choose life", as the Psalmist instructs us to do in the Bible. This is easily achievable, by asking Jesus to come into our hearts and by making Him our Lord and Saviour.

Not to make a choice is an unwise decision and disastrous. God has stated "want of knowledge has been the ruin of my people" (Hosea 4:6). It is so important that we make the right choice to ensure that our eternal destination is not hell, because of ignorance or unbelief. These two laws or kingdoms won't go away, whether you believe it or not, and Satan has the legal right of taking people who haven't made a choice with him, when he is thrown into the lake of fire at the end of the age. When people are unable to make a decision for themselves, another legally appointed person is allowed to make that decision for the person, and in this case, the legal person will be Satan, unless a choice has been made to accept Jesus as our advocate.

Chapter 8

Royal Law

Spiritual beings, such as humans, have spiritual laws which must be regarded seriously. We are constantly in the midst of a spiritual battle, and keeping God's laws enables God to be in control of all aspects of our lives that are not visible to our physical eyes, allowing Him (God) to intervene on our behalf. As a child of the Most High God you are recruited into the army of God, and therefore must look smart and follow the rule book of the army, as a loyal soldier. We cannot and must not slack off in any manner; we need to be good ambassadors to other fellow humans. We must be valiant soldiers ready for battle with our enemy, the devil, at all times. Keeping the Royal law gives us spiritual vision. There are spiritual laws that we must keep and make every effort to follow as spirit beings, which are created in the image of God; just as there are physical laws in our world like the law of gravity or the law of motion, they will have an effect.

- The Royal Law
- The Perfect Law of Liberty.

The Royal Law

It is the most essential common law of God, and yet it is the most important one too. "If, however you are observing the sovereign law laid down in scripture, 'Love your neighbour as yourself,' that is excellent (James 2:8.)

The Perfect Law of Liberty

This law requires born again spirit beings to hear the words of God and be doers of good works. "But he who looks into the perfect law, the law that makes us free, and does not turn away, remembers what he hears; he acts on it, and by so acting will find happiness." (James 1:25)

There are a series of requirements that the Perfect Law of Liberty demands.

"Discard everything sordid and every wicked excess, and meekly accept the message planted in your hearts, with its power to save you."(James 1:21)

(James 2:12) "Always **speak** and **act** as men who are to be judged under a law which makes them free."

We need to show mercy and speak God's word. Doing God's word or being doers of the word include:

- Controlling one's tongue and always being careful not to voice hurtful, harmful, damaging words.
- Visiting orphans and widows in their trouble, and helping them in their time of need.
- Keeping one's self unspotted from the world. To live a life of good moral standards, in every aspect of life; not partaking in any immoral way of life, and keeping well away from immorality

"If anyone thinks he is religious but does not bridle his tongue, he is deceiving himself; that man's religion is futile. A pure and faultless religion in the sight of God the Father is this: to look after orphans and widows in trouble and to keep oneself untarnished by the world" (James 1:26-27).

"Of that you may be certain, my dear friends. But everyone should be quick to listen, slow to speak, and slow to be angry. For human anger does not promote God's justice" (James1:19-20).

(James 2:22) "Surely you can see faith was at work in his actions, and by these actions his faith was perfected." So it is absolutely essential to have some action or 'works' before faith can manifest itself to perfection and bring about the desired things that one is believing God for or praying for.

'Speak only blessings'.

'Have good conduct' (James 3:10)

"Let him give practical proof of it by his right conduct, with the modesty of wisdom." (James 3:13)

We must not envy anyone or be self-seeking in any aspect. We must never lie about anything, and must never be boastful.

It is essential to be peace loving, considerate open-minded straightforward, sincere compassionate and kind.

There must be no partiality or hypocrisy in any of your dealings.

If we have shown mercy to other people and spoken God's word and obeyed Him and done His words or kept His commands then we will not be judged because "Mercy triumphs over judgement",(James 2:13).

Chapter 9

Special Treasure

Every human on planet earth is created in the image of God and we are all 'His possession' only because He made us, we therefore legally belong to Him. But because Adam sinned, and chose to follow the instructions of the devil rather than God, by disobeying God, by eating of the fruit of the tree, of the knowledge of good and evil, Adam lost his legal rights to dominate the earth, which was God's original plan. So the legal rights then became Satan's, as Adam had willingly crossed over into Satan's Kingdom by obeying Satan, rather than GOD. So because 'God's treasure', 'Adam', chose to move under the domain of another kingdom rule, therefore, he became a slave to Satan.

Now God did not leave the descendents of Adam there because of Adam's sin. God sent His Son Jesus, to pay the penalty of Adam's sin, with His blood and thus God purchased back the 'rights' for every human who then chooses to follow His Son Jesus, and accept Jesus in their Hearts; thus translating them from the kingdom of darkness; which belongs to Satan, into the Kingdom of God, which is the Kingdom of light.

The people who choose to accept Jesus, are now legally 'God's treasured possessions'. God specifically states in (Deuteronomy 7:6-8), "for you are a people holy to the Lord your God, and he has chosen you out of all peoples on earth to be His special possession", "because the Lord loved you." We must obey His commands and walk in His ways.

Treasured possessions are always under high security and kept in a safe place, wirelessly alarmed and well guarded. Similarly Christians are in an extremely safe place that is secure and well protected within high security measures. The Bible clarifies that we live within the shadow of the Almighty in the secret place of the God above all Gods, and that "the Angel of the Lord is on guard round those who fear Him and he rescues them" (Psalm 34:7).

So if you are a child of the Most High God, be assured that you have extremely High protection just like Fort Knox, and there are spiritual security cameras everywhere. Invisible beams of light in the spiritual realm, fence you in creating a secure area for you, a secret place, where no one can harm you or hurt you and get away. Spiritual High security circuits surround you, to protect you. "He who lives in the shelter of the Most High, who lodges under the shadow of the **Almighty**, says of the LORD, '**He** is my refuge and **fortress**" (Psalm 91:1-2).

The Angel of the Lord is described as a "mighty angel" (Revelation 10:1) Wow! Let your imagination run wild, and for extra comfort envision this mighty angel protecting you; because we are told that this Angel of God is settling in or establishing a camp, especially a military one around a child of God.(Proverbs 23:11) "a powerful Guardian who will take up their cause against you. The guard set on duty to protect every individual who is committed to Christ, is a gigantic military Angel. (Psalm 34:7) "The angel of the Lord is on guard round those who fear him and he rescues them". Our redeemer is Mighty.

As children of the most High God we must acknowledge the fact that we are God's treasured possessions, and rest assured, treasured possessions are always stored within strong, fortified, large buildings.

We must seriously renew our minds with the 'Word of God' and change our focus on to the things of God. It is every individual's choice to do what we want to do. We must not go against the will of God or violate the law of God, and break out of this high security protection, because in doing so, we would be putting ourselves at risk, from the enemy, who prowls about 'like a roaring lion'.

Do take note of the fact that the devil is not a roaring lion but only pretends to be like one. Only thieves move about restlessly and stealthily in search of prey; therefore anyone who is a child of God and breaks out of this high security system is putting themselves at extreme risk, because they are a target for the prowler. It would be the most foolish thing to do, and yet some people do these things in absolute ignorance. Anything precious that is out on the road is an easy target for violation and theft, and is vulnerable.

We are connected to the Most High God in the most intricate, complicated manner that humans can ever comprehend. We are so intricately and wonderfully made. The Lord watches over you, "the Lord is your guardian . . . . the Lord will guard you against all harm; He will guard your life. The Lord will guard you as you come and go, now and forever more" (Psalm 121:5, 7-8). "The Lord will rescue me from every attempt to do me harm, and bring me safely into His heavenly kingdom" (2 Timothy 4:17, 18). "Till you grow old I am the Lord, and when white hairs come, I shall carry you still; I have made you and I shall uphold you, I shall carry you away to safety" (Isaiah 46:4). "No one can snatch them out of my Father's care" (John 10:29). Invisible rays connect us directly to God; "You will **surround** them with favour as with a **shield**" (Psalm 5:12). He enfolds (surrounds or envelopes) us with light as with a garment. Anyone violating the continuity of those protective rays set off the alarms and is tracked and penalised. "The earth is full of your creatures." (Psalm 104:24). God's creatures are his riches that are his treasured possessions.

"For you are a people holy to the Lord your **God**, and he **has chosen you** out of all peoples on earth to be **his special possession**" (Deuteronomy 7:6).A special possession is a treasure, a very valuable object that is much loved or a highly valued person that is much loved as defined in human terms.

How much more must the God who created and formed us, hold us in high esteem and love each one of us?

Immensely.

Chapter 10

Patterns of Light and Sound

Sound and light go together, a perfect example being thunder and lightning. Both these make patterns on graphs if recorded, and have a mathematical formula or calculation, just like an Electro Cardiogram graph. Sounds in perfect harmony can soothe our souls and emotions in the form of song and music.

Sound or words have mathematical dimensions and different sounds make different patterns on graphs or have different mathematical structure. Humans speak different words that have different dimensions and structure that can be measured. How much more must Gods own words when spoken aloud have perfect structure and mathematical dimensions that make perfect beautiful spectacular patterns? The concept of Gods words, spoken aloud can be applied to practice to bring about perfect molecular structure in our human bodies, changing the imperfect mathematical calculations to perfect mathematical calculations, in molecular structure that may have been ravaged by disease to bring about perfect health and happiness.

(Proverbs 16:24) "**Kind words** are like dripping honey: sweetness to the palate and **health for the body**". God's words are like a honey comb, sweet to the soul and bringing health to the bones. A honey comb has many cells that are full of a sweet tasting substance, which is pleasurable to the taste and is also packed with healing properties. The cells in the honey comb have a perfect geometrical hexagonal shape and are innumerable in a single honey comb. These perfectly shaped cells are importantly storage containers, and similarly the Bible refers to our words as a honey comb dripping with sweet honey. Our spoken words (when we speak God's words) reshape every cell in our human body re-aligning them perfectly, just like the perfect shapes of cells in a honey comb. Our words are also containers like these storage cells of the honey comb, and we can fill these containers to bless ourselves as we speak, good words, and also to bless others or we can fill them with horrible words that will make horrible shapes for each cell in our body and also hurt others causing them distress.

Our spirits must be in subjection to our Heavenly Father, who is the Father of all spirits, in order that we may live. God's Spirit has made us, and God's breath gives us life. If God were to take away His Spirit and His breath from all of us, all the people would die together, and this flesh body would die and become dust (Job 34; 14) "If he were to turn his thoughts inwards and withdraw his life giving spirit, all flesh would perish on the instant, all mortals would turn again to dust."

God's Spirit of Understanding enables us to hear the sounds of God's Words. The Spirit of Understanding fine tunes the electrical and mechanical circuits in our bodies; literally tuning us into the same frequencies and wave lengths as God's radio frequencies, that enhance our hearing mechanism and enable us to decipher the sound of God's Words to an extent, that we are able to decipher clearly and differentiate the different sounds of His Words. By renewing our minds with His words, we are able to recognise His voice.

This fine tuning of our spirits can only take place when we choose to transform the electrical, mechanical and mathematical circuits in our spirits and bodies, by confessing the scriptures in God's Word daily. These Words when spoken aloud and confessed, make electrical and mathematical adjustments in our entire beings, opening us up, like a satellite dish to receive sound and light, making us receptors, and enabling us to decipher their pattern, and decode the sounds.

Sounds have patterns and light has patterns. Patterns of sound and light are recordable and can be measured on a graph and also made visible. God speaks to us in **light** because the Bible states that God is **Light**, so when we speak God's Words it acts as a satellite dish to receive Words from God which are in '**Light** form' and it is then converted and transmitted, in sound patterns to our minds, enabling us to decode the sound patterns and decipher the message to us, from God. By speaking God's Words it empowers our inbuilt satellite dish to receive the Spirit of Wisdom, and the Spirit of Understanding from our Creator, which is the decoder that switches on our capacity, to hear God's voice.

Chapter 11

The Will of God for Our Lives

When we accept Jesus in our hearts, our spirits are rekindled with the Holy Spirit of God, but our outer covering i.e. the human body, and our soul, need to be renewed as well, so as to line up with the things of God. So there are some important aspects of life that we have to deal with, in order to accomplish this completion of the new man; that the apostle Paul refers to in the Bible. Paul actually tells us what the will of God is, concerning this renewal of our vessels.

Containers or vessels which are hollow are used to contain fluid and for the conveying of blood and other bodily fluid; to conduct water and minerals. We are instructed to keep our vessels or our bodies pure.

"This is the will of God that you should be holy: you must abstain from fornication; each one of you must learn to gain mastery over his body, to hallow and honour it, not giving way to lust like the pagans who know nothing of God";(1 Thessalonians 4:3). It clearly specifies that God's will for our lives is our sanctification, and that we should abstain from sexual immorality. Purity of one's self is extremely important in this generation where sexual immorality is not considered as sexual immorality but is referred to as freedom to express one's sexuality and is encouraged in our society. Our young people are supported by policies and given advice on sexual health, and given the impression that everything is permissible, but all is against the will of God.

For most people in our world, God does not exist, and the devil has had a major success in tricking society into believing that it is alright to have sex out of wedlock, and that perversion and adultery is permissible. This is totally contradictory to God's will for our lives.

To achieve this aspect of godliness in our lives we have to take stock of our lives and make some minor or major changes ourselves, taking the first initial steps by ourselves; and God definitely gives us the grace that we require to accomplish this, sometimes with a lot of effort on our part. The Holy Spirit of God empowers us to be holy, just as God is Holy.

In order to accomplish the will of God in our lives 'and keep our vessels clean' we are told in the scriptures that we must not behave according to socially acceptable standards or conventions, but we must be transformed by the renewing of our minds (Romans 12:2) "Conform no longer to the pattern of this present world, but **be transformed by the renewal of your minds**. Then you will be able to discern the will of God and to know what is good and acceptable and perfect."

Renewing of our minds includes meditating on the Word of God, and meditating includes muttering along with ruminating and concentration. Transformation causes the undergoing of a marked change in physical appearance and form, "the skin of his face shone, because he had been talking with the LORD" (Exodus 34:29). Spending time in the presence of the Lord brings about changes in the voltage of the electric currents in our bodies also causing mathematical changes in the structures of the cells in our bodies. Our physical bodies consist of a large amount of water molecules and we are aware that sound vibrations create ripples and change the structure of water. Therefore the sound and vibrations of God's words spoken by us when we meditate on His Word in His

Presence change the mathematical structure of our body cells which consist of a large content of fluid. Transformation causes changes in structure mathematically.

So how does a person renew their mind and change the voltage currents in their bodies and make mathematical changes, in the entity of our spirits?

When we do not even know how to do these things and have no idea, that these things are actually present in our physical bodies; that there is an electrical system that has been put in place in our bodies by our Creator; and that our body does work on mathematical calculations, like a clock that is made with precise calculations to chime accurately on the hour.

Our body has been designed with a body clock that needs to eat, sleep, and rejuvenate, after all the waking hours of day. Similarly our spirit and soul that live in this human body must be transformed in electric currents and have their voltage changed and undergo mathematical changes. We do not know the complicated mathematical calculations, to keep this extremely intelligent gadget 'the human body' running, perfectly; but we are clearly told what we must do to achieve this, and so in faith we must renew our minds every day by speaking the words of God; and confessing it aloud as often as we can, every single day of our lives.

By doing so, we also grow our faith, because faith comes by hearing, and as we speak God's words aloud every day, we are able to hear, what we are saying, and it enters our spirits and soul. Even though we may not realise it, just like a plant that is watered, which soon grows healthy and strong; similarly our spirit, soul and body are changed by the nourishment of the "Word" making them healthy and whole, and causes healing to our entire being.

When we confess the Word of God regularly, it automatically makes the necessary changes in the flow of electricity, and the mathematical calculations, in our bodies, to transform us into new creations. We can then live in the world physically and yet have a 'spiritual might', to easily refuse and refrain from anything that is evil. We are strengthened and enabled to walk a good Christian life without being contaminated by the things of the world. In other words we develop the ability to say 'no', to what we know is wrong, without much effort.

So if you have an illness, then just confess the healing scriptures that are there in the Bible; freely available for our healing and it will change the mathematical calculations and electric voltage of the currents in your body to '**healing mode**'. For any changes that you may require to make in your life, you can find verses in the Bible that relate to the situation, and confess them, constantly, thus applying them to bring about the required changes in your circumstances. **God's words** can be applied to any aspect of life to change your situation, as the power in God's words changes the voltage in electrical currents and restructures mathematical calculations; without us even knowing how we are doing complicated calculations, and tampering with the electrical system of the universe.

As we speak God's Words, they become the power switches in our world; that the world cannot access or tamper with unless they are wired up to the Creator God through His Son Jesus. But we have legal access to all these switches in our world, and we can only activate these when the voltage currents of our minds are tuned in to the same electrical field or circuits of our Father God. There are powerful magnetic fields in the world and in our human body that control our well being, and these can be reset, when we speak God's words. Bible verses when spoken aloud are positive words that make our physical brain send out positive command signals to every cell in our body telling them to cause positive outcomes. When we speak negative words they put our body into 'destruction mode'. So it is essential to speak the right words to create a perfect field of magnetic current, and energy; for everything to work positively for us.

The devil does not have access to these power switches and cannot make any changes in the electrical circuits or any mathematical changes in our body clocks unless we give him access with our negative words, and so he is helpless if we do not give him any words. Therefore, we ought to obey God's instructions, to guard our mouths, and our hearts, because they are important to ensure life more abundantly (Proverbs 4:23-24) "Guard your heart . . . . for it is the source of all life." "Keep your mouth from crooked speech and banish deceitful talk from your lips."The Godly principle of applying God's words practically can be used to change your situation, by speaking positive words only.

Never mind what the symptoms are or what the reality of any situation maybe, we are given the authority by God to use His words to change the situation and the electrical currents that will bring about change when spoken out loud constantly, never changing your words, no matter how negative things may look like at that moment. You can turn your world around positively, by using God's words, and you have the legal right to do so.

We are power houses of electricity; and we do not even know this. The apostle Paul tells us that we shine as lights in this world, in the middle of a corrupt and perverse generation (Philippians 2:15) "Show yourselves innocent and above reproach, faultless children of God in a crooked and depraved generation in which **you shine** like stars in a dark world." Light requires an electrical circuit to function accurately.

God's words are a declaration, to be uttered; they are the basic units of data that are required to transform our lives. They are complex passwords that have a specific function, they are signals, and commands that make everything operate perfectly. We create the circuits around us by what we are saying each day. We can speak the circuits of the things that we need, into existence, by speaking words that create the electrical circuit for it to be transported by, from the spiritual world into the physical world.

Spoken words create a conveyor belt, which we initiate to transfer all that we require from the spiritual world into our physical world. This is why we are instructed in the Bible to call the things that we need, into existence because we have to first speak into existence the conveyor belt for the thing that we require to be transferred or transported to us from God.

Everything that we need is already present in the spirit world. This is why at creation, God first made 'light' because it is the basic requirement for the existence of all things. Everything in our universe, functions in circuits and circles or cycles. Nothing grows without light, if light were taken away from our planet, it would be at a standstill. We have so much power available to us at the tip of our tongues, to make our lives and journey on this planet a prosperous, victorious one. If only we can control our tongues, and always use the right words; because negative words cause a break in the electrical circuit. This is why we are instructed in the book of James not to doubt, as it makes a person to speak negative words, which stops the movement of the conveyor belt, interrupting the process, causing one not to receive anything.

God's light is on the inside of us, and it isn't just a tiny flickering candle, as we imagine it. It is light bursting forth from our Father's face, powerful light, the same light that ignites the sun, powerful laser beams—electromagnetic rays with a powerful voltage.

Have we ever questioned electric currents in our body and where they come from?

There is obviously a source, because we do know that our hearts and brains work on electric currents, since we measure them; in the form of Electro-Cardiograms and Electro-Encephalograms; this is God's 'light 'in each one of us, that is the power source.

When we confess God's words, we are able to flick on the spiritual power line switch, which is high voltage current or electricity that burns out impurities, just like laser technology—blasting for e.g.; kidney or bladder stones. God's light floods our being, burning out the dross, and all the impure cells in our physical bodies, giving us good health. Visualize this great burst of light power, flooding your body as you confess God's word, because in reality that is what happens in your spirit.

Our spirit gets lit by God's Spirit on the inside of our body (our house-vessel) and light comes shining out of our windows like the light from a lighthouse, shining bright on a dark night. This is similar to low voltage current that flows quietly doing all the gentle, everyday tasks; high voltage currents are used for powerful tasks that require a very high voltage.

We must have a forgiving heart when we confess God's words. Any unforgiveness or grudges or past hurts that we hold on to could cause a barrier between you and God, and stop the flow of blessings. We must love the unlovely and always forgive one another. Use God's love to break down walls and barriers.

We are "Holy people" to the Lord our God, and He has chosen us to be His special treasure, because He loves us.

The things of this life are temporary and are passing away, so do not set your heart on the things of this world, but give priority to the things of God, that take us into the spirit world, which is real and exists alongside our world, even though we are unable to see it. It is the spirit of man that is of utmost importance and that will live on forever, if we walk in God's will and way, on this earth. We also need to line up our lives with the Word of God, in order to receive the blessings that have been promised to us here. Just as, for it to rain on us, we have to get out in the rain.

Peter tells us that "God's divine power has bestowed on us everything that makes for life and true religion" (2 Peter 1:3); or the capacity to live a godlike life, having the same properties and characteristics of our Creator, God. Micah 3:8 specifies that by the Spirit of the Lord "I am full of strength, of justice and power." For perfection, "Finally to bind everything together and complete the whole there must be love." (Colossians 3:14). Love is the thing used to fasten or tie things together to the Lord, making an agreement with legal force, that makes faith work; just like (Galatians 5:6) "The only thing that counts is faith expressing itself through love". So when we speak God's words in love, they work definitely, because it is bound to the Lord; and it is the Creator speaking through us.

Chapter 12

Essential Ingredients for a Spirit Filled Life: Righteousness

Righteousness is an important requirement, for the "Spirit of Wisdom, Knowledge and Understanding" to be able to dwell and function within our spirits. The prophet Isaiah prophesied that the people of the world would learn righteousness; "the inhabitants of the world learn what justice is" (Isaiah 26:9), indicating that this is a subject that has to be learned, to be perfected.

When we receive Jesus as our personal saviour, we receive the righteousness of God, and God directs our ways; and no more does God see our sin, because He blots them out and He sees us through Jesus, who is the righteousness of God. This gives us no excuse, because we must still learn so as to line up our lives to correspond with the Word of God; and live a fulfilled, complete life in the Spirit, as God destined us to do.

We must not settle for, and be content with the bare minimum in life; as we really are 'super humans', as God designed us to be. It is simply the training process that is required to bring out the best in us, and equip us to use all that is provided to us, in the spirit. Just like we need to go to school as we grow, when we are children, to learn the things of this world; so when we are spiritually reborn we need to learn and grow to be professionals in the spirit, and this requires training. We need to learn from our parent, Father God (Abba, Father), the Holy Spirit by spending time daily in His presence. Bible schools and human teachers are available to assist us.

People who have a right standing with God can practice 'righteousness', in a similar manner to that of God who is righteous. "Anyone who does what is right is righteous, just as Christ is righteous" (1John 3:7). Those who make peace actually sow righteousness, making it like a seed, that when sown will eventually grow and produce good fruit, and bring a sure reward. "Peace is the seed-bed of righteousness, and peacemakers will reap its harvest" (James 3:18). Making peace does not just mean the Nobel prize winners, it includes every one of us who in our daily lives, hold our tongue when we are provoked by the issues of life, that make us angry, and overlook faults of other people that upset us. These are the real Nobel Prize winners, who daily keep the peace in any situation.

By speaking the truth always, we are actually declaring righteousness. Righteousness is a road that leads to life; 'eternal life'. "Anyone set on righteousness finds life" (Proverbs 11:19). A person who is righteous does not tell lies "Right conduct protects the honest" (Proverbs 13:6).

When a person spends time in the Word of God they are able to learn the righteousness that is so vital for life; and when they have learnt this, and are able to successfully practice this in daily living, it has the ability to deliver them from death and also give them guidance daily, ensuring that they are on the right path. Through constant practice of right living, people are able to accomplish righteousness, just like our Creator God, is righteous. The way to ensure that we always walk righteously is to always confess that we have righteousness and strength; and say "In the Lord alone are victory and might" (Isaiah 45:24). Personalizing the verse, by inserting your name in it; applies and connects the principle directly to you, bringing about the desired effect and outcome.

When we are born of God, we must do all that is in our capacity to keep away from even the temptation of sin, so as not to grieve God. It upsets and grieves human parents when their children go astray and make the wrong choices; similarly it also makes God sad to see His children wandering from the path of life.

There are two kinds of spirits that we must be able to identify and differentiate in this world.
- The Spirit of Truth.
- The spirit of error.

The **Spirit of Truth** is from God, and is the genuine Spirit, and we receive this Spirit from God so that we are enabled to know the **things** of God, that have been freely given to us by God. "We have received this Spirit from God, not the spirit of the world, so that we may know all that God has lavished on us" (1 Corinthians 2:12).

What are these things that have been freely given to us by God?

Paul the apostle tells us that these '**things**' are:

- Tender mercies
- Kindness
- Humility
- Meekness
- Longsuffering
- Bearing with one another
- Forgiving one another
- Love.

Above all things, the most important one is **love,** and we are instructed to put this on, because it is the **bond of perfection**. It is the connection with God, the direct line of contact that is a vital link, which binds us securely to our Creator. These things correspond with the fruits of the Holy Spirit of God, which are "love, joy, peace, patience, kindness, goodness, fidelity, gentleness, and self-control. Against such things is no law". (Galatians 5:22-23)

Putting on love is like literally putting on a garment and it requires some effort to do this. Sometimes we may find ourselves in a situation where we may completely dislike a person for how inconsiderate they are, or how difficult they are, and yet we have to be nice to them; and it is extremely difficult and uncomfortable for us to be nice. Yet God requires us to put on this garment of love; not for the benefit of the other person, but for the benefit of ourselves, so that our bond with God may be perfected, making us stronger in the Lord and thus benefitting us. We may find this so annoying to do under these circumstances, and yet it still remains the vital ingredient for perfection of the bond, that our spirit so desperately requires, to be strong."**Put on then garments that suit God's chosen and beloved people: compassion, kindness, humility, gentleness, patience. Be tolerant with one another and forgiving.**" (Colossians3:12-13)

(1 John 4:6) "We can distinguish the Spirit of Truth from the **spirit of error**". The **spirit of error** is the counterfeit spirit, that is demonic, and this is why we are advised to test the spirits. This spirit of error is prevalent and rampant in our world, and causes and entices people to live life irresponsibly and rashly, which eventually leads to various addictions and health problems. The major characteristic of this spirit is hate.

So how do we test these spirits?

These spirits can be tested by taking note of their characteristics or the 'things' that are manifested in comparison to the things of the Spirit of God. Their characteristics would be the complete opposite to tender mercies, kindness, humility, meekness, longsuffering, bearing with one another, forgiving one another, and love.

(Isaiah 32:17) "Righteousness will yield peace, and bring about quiet trust forever"."

Vessels are often talked about in the scriptures, for example vessels of clay, earthen vessels, chosen vessels, vessels of gold and silver, vessels that are precious, and vessels of honour, vessels of mercy, and vessels of wrath. The bible even says that the vessels of wrath are created for the day of destruction. Vessels in context here are human containers, and all containers have an opening, and the outer most part of any opening in a container would be called the lips of a container or vessel. Vessels can contain substance or **things** and can be used for storage. There is always only a particular amount of substance that a vessel can store depending on the size or capacity of the vessel.

Vessels are made by a potter; they cannot just come into existence, without being made. It is the potters choice as to what shape he makes the vessel, and whether He makes just an ordinary one or whether he makes a very well crafted beautiful one. He is able to use a lump of clay on the potter's wheel to make whatever he chooses. But whatever vessel he creates or makes, be it a beautiful one or be it a not so beautiful one, all the vessels will have an opening, and the openings to any sort of containers are called Lips, which are always the outer most part of a vessel. The size of the container depends upon the potter, it is his choice to make a small container or a very large one, and depending on the size of the container, the volume of substance that every container can hold will differ. The potter has the power to make what he chooses; the lump of clay in his hand has no choice at all to choose what shape it would like to be moulded into.

Similarly the Bible informs us that God is the potter, and He has made vessels of wrath and vessels of mercy. The vessels of wrath are vessels that are created for the day of destruction (Romans 9:22) "**Vessels** that were **objects of retribution** due for destruction". There are vessels of mercy which God had prepared before hand for glory. (Romans 9:23 "**Vessels** that were **objects of mercy**, prepared from the first for glory. **We are those objects of mercy, whom He has called**".

Every time the scriptures talk about vessels it is in reference to the masterpiece of creation that is discussed: humans! So if humans are referred to as containers, and have an opening called lips, it is what we fill into these containers that will come out of our lips. We need to gorge ourselves on spiritual food, not physical food, in order to have a happy fulfilled life. Good words, God's words are spiritual food that we must fill into our data banks (our soul brain and physical brain); by memorising scriptures from the Bible, for good words to overflow all the time from our mouths when we speak.

Containers have a limited capacity, and when it is full, there is no other way that the substance in that container can still remain inside; it has to overflow. So that what is in the container will spill out, and hence the outcome is familiar, because out of the abundance of all that is stored in you in word format, will come pouring out from your mouth. Similar to a cup that is filled up and will overflow if filled to the brim; even so if we are joyful spirits, it will overflow to others.

Everybody is a different type and sized container depending on how our Creator designed us and made us. Our vessel, the human body, contains the spirit of the person with the soul, and the Holy Spirit of God. It is up to us what we fill in our containers, and we are given instructions as to what we should fill in our containers, and that is the words of God. If we fill it up with good things, then good things will spill out, when we overflow, but if we constantly fill rubbish into our containers then rubbish will spill out when we are full to the overflow. If **good things** (i.e. goodness, kindness, meekness etc) spill out of our lives we are able to be a blessing to others, but if rubbish flows out of our containers then it is of no use to anyone and actually that makes the vessel, useless.

A waste of space and time to have rubbish around isn't it?

A rubbish vessel becomes fit only for incineration, a 'vessel of wrath' for destruction.

Proverbs 8:7-8 declares "I speak nothing but the truth and my lips detest wicked talk." Only right things can come from our mouths and from the opening of our lips, and all our words will be spoken in righteousness, when we allow the spirit of Wisdom to live on the inside of us.

Proverbs 8:12 says "I am Wisdom; I bestow shrewdness and show the way to knowledge and discretion." Visualize, Wisdom, who is a Spirit dwelling in our spirits, that lives together with prudence in the human body, that has lips. This vessel now contains, right things, because

Wisdom has the right words in her vessel. These right things then come out of her (Wisdom's) mouth, accompanied by righteousness. So when a person obtains the Spirit of Wisdom; She (Wisdom) dwells in the person, enabling that person to create right things, because the Spirit of Wisdom enhances the person's speech centre to speak the right things into existence. Clearly Wisdom is a spirit person and refers to herself as 'I', and dwells or lives inside a person. So Wisdom and prudence dwell together side by side within a person and together they find out knowledge and discretion.

The human body, or vessel, can contain other spirits too, along with our own spirit. This makes it seem like a great big room on the inside of each one of us that has the capacity to accommodate our spirit, the Holy Spirit and also room for seven other spirits. If we do not allow the Holy Spirit to dwell in us along with the seven other Spirits of God i.e. Wisdom, Knowledge, Understanding, Counsel, Might and Fear of the Lord, then this space in our spirits or vessels is unoccupied space or vacant accommodation. If we are not careful, squatters will take over this empty space in our vessels; just like the squatters in this world who don't have any scruples, and are dominant and take things by force. These spiritual squatters are the demon spirits that are looking for vessels, because they do not have vessels of their own.

Jesus warns us of these pirate spirits, when He said "when an unclean spirit comes out of someone it wanders over the desert sands" (Matthew 12:43).

"It goes off and collects seven other spirits more wicked than itself, and they all come in and settle there; and in the end that person's plight is worse than before. That is how it will be with this wicked generation".

(Matthew12:45, Luke 11:26); clearly demonstrating that our human body or vessel has enough room in the vessel to house at least seven spirits, whether they are good or bad.

Equipped with this knowledge, we ought to be extremely vigilant, as we are also warned by God, that the devil is like a roaring lion seeking whom he may devour. The word 'seeking' identifies that one has to seek out a home or a dwelling place for the physical body to live, in this world. Similarly in the spirit world, demon spirits seek out a dwelling place or a body or a vessel (house) for the spirit to live. We are truly super humans created by God Almighty, spiritual beings that are masterpieces. We are wonderfully made. The Lord refers to His children or those who have accepted Jesus into their hearts (vessels) as 'chosen vessels', or instruments that are commissioned to take the gospel of Jesus to every person: "My chosen instrument to bring my name before the nations and their kings." (Acts 9:15).

Vessels or human bodies that don't contain God's Spirit are extremely vulnerable vessels. They contain their own spirit, which does not have the 'things' of God, and are open to host demon spirits unknowingly. These demon spirits have their own doctrines, so we must always be aware of these deceiving spirits and their doctrines, as Satan is a counterfeit, and even tries to counterfeit God's Spirit and sometimes succeeds in deceiving people; even God's people. Those who do not have the Spirit of Knowledge, and have not renewed their minds with the Word of God; these are the gullible ones as they are actually unable to recognise what is counterfeit, because they do not know the original at all.

Hence it is so important for us to renew our minds, with the Word of God, so as to recognise the Holy Spirit and differentiate Him, from the counterfeit spirit of the devil. The Bible cautions us; that "Satan himself masquerades as an angel of light" (2 Corinthians 11:14). We are even warned to beware of people, tricksters pretending to be Christian apostles. We can recognise these imposters by their fruits, or their deeds, and their speech.

(Zech 12:1) "Lord . . . . formed the spirit of mortals". It is our Creator God who gives our spirits a form. At creation, the form that God gave to human spirits was 'His image'; and He confirmed this in the book of Genesis.

(Num 16:22) "God of the **spirits of all mankind**"; or the God of the **spirits of all humans (flesh),** confirms that these spirits that God created live in a flesh body; clarifying our thoughts about who is the real me. In the Bible, Job knew who he was because he said "the Spirit of God made me, the breath of the Almighty gave me life" (Job 33:4). There is a spirit in man; Job definitely knew that what he was talking about was true, without a doubt.

When God anoints us in the spirit with the 'oil of gladness'(Psalm 45:7) and the 'oil of joy'(Isaiah 61:3); our human bodies which are containers get filled up and start overflowing to bless others. Just like a fountain that is full of water, which is pushed out under pressure and comes bursting forth out of its mouth, causing a spray of water that is both beautiful to look at and also cool and refreshing. Our lives can be compared similarly, when we are able to refresh others with our good words and kind deeds and what comes pouring out of our spirits.

(Psalm 45:7) "You love right and hate wrong; therefore God, your God, has anointed you above your fellows with oil, the token of joy". When we love righteousness, and hate wickedness and lawlessness, God then gives and anoints us with the oil of gladness. He blesses us forever, and makes us exceedingly glad with His presence. The oil of gladness is His presence. (Psalm 21:6) "You . . . make him glad with the joy of your presence". We are anointed with the oil of gladness more than our companions, and we are filled with His presence in our vessels, so much so we are always happy and content with His blessings.

Chapter 13

Spiritual Garments

The spiritual man is provided with garments, just like our physical man, is provided with clothes and it is we, who have to make an effort to put these on, just like we put our clothes on daily. These garments can be compared to, our high street fashion designer clothing, that many love to shop for. There is a very high price to pay for designer clothing. We could agree to settle for less expensive clothing which is also easily available and inexpensive, but it is always a counterfeit for a designer wear article. There are lots of different types of garments which are mentioned in the Bible which are not ideal for human spirits.

There are a variety of garments available for the spirit man, and to acquire and put these on requires effort on our part; in the flesh body, and also effort in the spirit man. Commencement of this effort requires to begin with diligently confessing God's words daily, whereby we are transformed by the Word. Literally, the electrical circuits in our body get restructured, by our Creator God when we confess His Words. This restructuring is the foundation that God builds upon, as we confess 'His Word' and grow in His words.

The initial most important garment that our spirit needs and that we are told to put on is the **garment of Salvation**, which is, **Jesus Christ**. There is a garment of praise, a garment of righteousness, white garments, white robes dipped in the blood of the lamb, and a garment of love. The Blood signifies the blood of our Lord Jesus Christ that cleanses us from all sin. God is "enfolded in a robe of light" (Psalm 104:2). There is a 'garment of darkness' which we must first **cast off** to be able to put on the "armour of Light" (Romans 13:12).

We have been freely given 'things' by God. Many imagine 'things' to be material goods to delight our fleshly desires, such as television sets, cars, mobile phones, houses and all the other things that the carnal (worldly) man desires. But God is talking about "things" that are essential and absolutely necessary for our spirit, because these things are eternal. These are designer wear spiritual garments that we can put on. These garments are originals, manufactured by our Creator, they are royal robes that cannot be purchased in a cheap regular store; but come from the store house of heaven with designer labels, that have the trademark of our Father God, Jesus Christ and the Holy Spirit.

These are "things" that the spirit person can choose to put on and must choose to put on, in order to live a life worthwhile and pleasing to God. These 'things' are given to us, free of cost when we put on Christ. These "things" are spiritual garments that have super power from our Creator which empowers our spirits to grow and live life in this world successfully, achieving our goals. "Fix your thoughts on that higher realm, not on this earthly life" (Colossians 3:1). Concentrate and set your attention and desires on **things above**, not on things of the earth. "Put on, then, **garments** that suit God's chosen and beloved people: compassion, kindness, humility, gentleness, patience. Finally to **bind everything** together and complete the whole, there must be **love**." (Colossians 3:12, 14)

These spiritual things or garments that our spirits need to live and grow are:

- Tender mercies
- Kindness
- Humility
- Meekness
- Long suffering
- Bearing with one another
- Forgiving one another
- Love

These are essential spiritual garments. Just like our physical body needs food; not just any rubbish food, but proper nutritious food, to grow healthy and strong; similarly our spirit person needs the things of the spirit, which is food for our spirits, to grow healthy and strong. A wicked ungodly lifestyle is like trash food and will destroy the body and spirit and soul of a person.

Love is the greatest, most important **thing**, or garment. Imagine putting on a Jesus suit or garment, and then being able to receive "things" which make us grow, and give us access into the spirit world, from where we can call physical things into reality, by strengthening these "things" with words from the Bible. This is a reality, because when we receive Jesus in our hearts and spirits, He is the doorway into the spirit world and the Kingdom of God; and the throne room of heaven where we are seated with God in heavenly places. So if we are seated with Christ in the throne room of heaven, we can command our situations in life by using the authority and power of the name of Jesus; because every knee in heaven and on earth and under the earth must bow to the name of Jesus.

We should not and must not change or exchange these designer label clothes from God for any counterfeit clothing, and we must not take off our spiritual clothing (i.e. tender mercies, kindness, and humility, meekness, longsuffering, bearing with one another, forgiving one another and love). These spiritual clothes must be worn at all times in layers that grow on us, turning it into spiritual armour as the layers grow thicker (in life situations, when we learn to stand fast and endure). These things bring temporary suffering in our present world, but also teach us obedience and endurance which leads to perfection. Paul the apostle tells us to put on the whole armour of God, the helmet of salvation, the breast plate of righteousness, the belt of truth, the sword of the Spirit (which is the 'Word of God'), shield of faith, and feet shod with the gospel of peace.

We can make a lot of effort to be dressed smartly spiritually, just as we can physically; depending on what type of garments we wear. We are warned not to put on two types of spiritual garments that are very harmful for us and dangerous. These two garments are the garments of vengeance and the garments of violence. Awareness of these two garments is essential and important, so as to avoid these dangerous spiritual attires that can harm us spiritually and ruin us, completely.

The garment of vengeance is when we try to avenge ourselves when someone has hurt us or wronged us. We are clearly instructed not to put on a garment of vengeance; but to let things go, and commit the situation to God', because "Vengeance is mine, says the Lord, I will repay" (Romans 12:19).

The garment of violence would include any malicious violent thoughts, malicious gossip, harsh words, foul language, and physically violent activity. God also includes divorce as a garment of violence; cautioning us not to put it on; as it can cause a human soul and spirit to be vulnerable to attacks from the enemy, who could destroy a human soul and spirit.

Jesus councils us to buy gold from Him that is refined in the fire, so that we may be rich, and white garments that we may be clothed, that the shame of our nakedness may not be seen. We are told in Revelation 3:18 to apply "ointment for your eyes so that you may see" and perceive **spiritual things**. The 'ointment' which Jesus is talking about, with which to anoint our eyes, is His "Name" (Song of Songs 1:3) In simple words, Jesus is telling us to keep our focus on Him at all times.

White garments are spiritual clothing which are a dire necessity, so that "the shame of your nakedness, may not be revealed" (Rev 3:18). When we are spiritually naked, we are very vulnerable to predators, very much similarly, as if we went about naked in the natural world. We would be vulnerable, and it would be shameful.

The spiritual world around us is real, existing alongside our physical world, and it can be very intimidating when demon spirits manifest themselves in different ways and can be heard, felt or seen. This is why it is essential to clothe our spirit man so that we are not vulnerable to these demon spirits. We can be frightened and even terrified by these demon spirits, whose only aim is to steal, kill and destroy. These demon spirits are fallen angels who rebelled against God and were cast out of heaven.

Guess where they landed?

You're right! Planet earth! This is their domain for a limited amount of time until the return of Jesus Christ to his earth.

When we accept Jesus in our hearts, by confessing with our mouths, we become new creatures in our spirits, because God's Spirit, gives us life; but we are told that we must cast off darkness or the **garment of darkness** and put on **light** which is also a garment, and a very powerful strong garment; it is royal designer wear, that is also referred to, as the **armour of Light**. We are instructed to put on the Lord Jesus Christ. **"Let Christ Jesus himself be the armour that you wear: give your unspiritual nature no opportunity to satisfy its desires" (Rom 13:14)**. Jesus is also a spiritual garment that we put on by confessing His words everyday and are empowered to endure and overcome temptations. Jesus suits can only be purchased from one shop, and this is the King's shop in heaven; and the currency to obtain this powerful Jesus garment, is our lives surrendered to Him.

The Bible differentiates clothes from garments, clothes cover the flesh body of a person; and garments cover the spirit part of a person. A perfect example is the story of Joseph. When Joseph went to his brothers, they stripped him of his tunic of many colours and threw him in the pit, and when his brother Reuben had returned to the pit and found that Joseph was not there he tore his clothes. His father Jacob also tore his clothes on news about his son Joseph. The tearing of one's physical clothes that cover the flesh part of our body, signifies (in the Bible) grief and mourning. Whereas tearing or rending one's garments; refers to spiritual attire being painstakingly taken off in repentance, with a yearning for ridding oneself of sin and casting off garments of spiritual sin or darkness. This is a painful process, as humans get comfortable with sin and even take pleasure in it; and there is a choice to make when a person repents; to rend or tear off this spiritual garment of darkness and sin, to exchange it for a garment of light; which takes a lot of human effort. But His grace is enough for us to do this; it is achievable, not in our own strength but with God's grace and favour. We are enabled and assisted to exchange our garments. There is a choice to be made first by each one of us, to enable this process.

Revelation 16: 15 alert us to heed instruction and be aware of the times, preparing us for the return of Christ to the earth; "See I am coming like a thief! Happy the man who stays awake", and keeps his garments clean "so that he will not have to go naked and ashamed for all to see!" Keeping our spiritual garments clean is an absolute requirement of the Spiritual law of God.

Chapter 14

Wisdom

In the unseen spiritual world around us, there are two categories of wisdom. These spiritual categories are dominated by spirit beings that exist; and affect our lives, depending on which spirit we permit to enter into our spirit.

> **Heavenly Wisdom**. (Heavenly Spirit, which is one of the seven Spirits of God mentioned in the book of Isaiah and Revelation.)
>
> **Demonic wisdom** (Demonic spirit)

Heavenly Wisdom: Descends "from above is in the first place pure; and then peace-loving, considerate, and open-minded; it is straightforward and sincere, rich in compassion and in deeds of kindness that are its fruits" (James 3:17). This spirit is a very gentle spirit person and will prompt and guide us, but never controls a person, and always allows one to make their own choices. Wisdom from God makes the person a very kind, loving, gentle personality, who is sensitive to the needs of others around. The Spirit of Wisdom enhances a person's life in every aspect; making positive changes with positive outcomes.

Demonic wisdom: "This is not the wisdom that comes from above; it is earth-bound sensual, demonic" (James 3:15). There is bitter envy and self-seeking, in one's heart, boasting and lying against the truth. Confusion and all evil works accompany Envy and Strife, who are two demon spirits. Anything that appeals to the five human senses, i.e. taste, touch, smell, sight, and hearing; and does not line up with God's word, is demonic.

A person should stay away from these things; for example the wrong kind of music or swearing, or the television programmes that do not glorify God, e.g. pornography, or even simple programmes that have a lot of swear words, or inappropriate pictures that you would not sit and watch with your parents. An example of taste is alcohol, drugs, smoking. Example of touch would most definitely be sex out of marriage, or before marriage. These things would fall into the category of demonic wisdom, because they are sensual.

This worldly wisdom is a demon spirit that controls humans when they permit these demon spirits into their lives, for example: people become slaves to drugs and alcohol, and the demon spirit then controls their actions :making them to do the things they would never want to do, it causes them to be violent, difficult beings who are abusive.

Therefore now that we are aware of the devil's counterfeit 'wisdom' we can be aware and know the signs that signify demonic wisdom and are able to differentiate and beware, so that we are not fooled in any manner.

Moving on to the Wisdom of God we will gain an insight into all that we as Christians ought to know and have, so that we are not fooled, because the Bible specifically warns that God's people are destroyed because of their inadequate knowledge. To ensure we have adequate knowledge we must read, listen and obey God's words.

Wisdom of God:

The Bible instructs us to get wisdom.

How does one get wisdom?

The answer to this is also in the Bible where we are told that "the first step to wisdom is the fear of the LORD, and knowledge of the Most Holy One is understanding" (Proverbs 9:10).

So what is this 'wisdom 'that is an absolute necessity in life, that we are instructed in our instruction manual, the Bible, to get?

"Grasp **God's secret**, which is **Christ himself**, in whom lie hidden all the **treasures** of **wisdom** and knowledge" (Col 2:3)

'Wisdom 'is clearly one of the seven Spirits of God that are mentioned in the book of Revelation, and is always referred to as a "She" (Proverbs 9:1-3) throughout the Bible.

The Holy Spirit, is always referred to in the Bible as 'He' (Here we clearly can see the male and female components or spirits that God put into man when He created the spirit man in His image; and stated that "male and female He created them"; this was before the man out of dust was made or even before Eve was made.)

We very clearly have to ask God for Wisdom and the Holy Spirit, because the Bible clearly specifies that God **gives** Wisdom. "It is the LORD who bestows wisdom and teaches knowledge and understanding" (Proverbs 2:6) therefore to be given something we have to **ask,** because again we are clearly instructed "If any of you lacks wisdom he should ask God and it will be given him" (James 1:5). Wisdom (who is also one of the Seven Spirits of God) is able to abide, reside and inhabit human spirits when we ask God for Wisdom. We are instructed to ask in faith without doubting. There are other Spirits i.e. "the seven Spirits of God," (Revelation 5:6), and these are:

- The Holy Spirit,
- The Spirit of Wisdom
- The Spirit of understanding
- The Spirit of counsel
- The Spirit of might
- The Spirit of knowledge
- The Spirit of the fear of the Lord

(Isaiah 11:2) "On him the Spirit of the Lord will rest: a spirit of wisdom and understanding, a spirit of counsel and power, a spirit of knowledge and fear of the Lord.

These '**seven Spirits of God**, are "the **eyes** which are the seven spirits of God sent to every part of the world" (Revelation 5:6). In (Zechariah 4:10) "these seven, he said are the eyes of the Lord which range over the whole earth." These seven spirits **scan** the whole earth with their eyes, and they rejoice to see. These seven Spirits are rejoicing Spirits, or rather have the ability to rejoice, and they also have the ability to see, because they are described as the eyes of the Lord, which scan.

An exciting awareness that these seven Spirits of God can see and scan; make the connection with the creation story, where interestingly, God made man in his own **image**. When humans create an image it can only be produced or reproduced by the method of scanning. When God created 'man' He said 'let (allow to escape) US', indicating that He allowed light and the components of God to escape from His face, eyes. He was able to create man in His image using the Light or electromagnetic radiation by the Holy Spirit or as the Bible states "the Spirit of God was hovering over the face of the waters."(Genesis 1:1)

The seven Spirits of God have vision like scanning machines which in simple terms means, a very powerful vision; because nothing escapes from the eye of the scanner, all is visible and nothing can be hidden, right to the innermost cells of our body. The depths of the earth are visible to these seven Spirits of God, so there is nothing that any man does, and no place that anyone may go, that is not visible to God, because these scanners '**scan the whole earth**'.

God gives the Spirit of Wisdom, and that is when Wisdom enters your heart. Wisdom can only enter when the (Spirit of) Fear of the Lord is dwelling on the inside of you.

So what does it mean to fear the Lord?

"To fear the LORD is to hate evil. Pride, arrogance, evil ways, subversive talk" (Proverbs 8:13). We have to make a lot of effort to correct and root out some of the unwanted habits we have encouraged and permitted to dominate our lives. Initially, as we begin to cut out the things that do not impress or please God in any aspect, it is difficult and painful. All this is worth the effort because Wisdom can then function in us and direct our lives and give us instruction. These instructions we are able to comprehend and follow, since our receptors are then freed up of all the garbage that we had allowed the world to dump on us. De-cluttering our lives of worldly mannerisms; that do not edify or enhance our lives makes room for the Spirit of Wisdom to enter into our spirits. It can be similarly compared to receptors in our human brain that get cluttered with whatever we feed them with, and get addicted to that substance; which one then has to detoxify or clear out the substance, in order to free up the receptors, before we can replace them with a better substance. "He (God) gives wisdom to the wise" (Daniel 2:21).

God gives His wisdom only to the wise. He gives the Spirit of Wisdom and He also gives the Spirit of Might, and both these Spirits together make known to us anything we may have asked God about. He removes kings and appoints other kings in their place with the Spirit of Might; and He changes the times and seasons with the Spirit of Wisdom. He reveals deep and secret things with the Spirit of knowledge and the Spirit of understanding. "With Him light has its dwelling" (Daniel 2:22). Here' light 'is referring to the conspicuous person (Jesus), and these seven Spirits are hidden in Jesus.

Daniel was a wise man in the sight of God, and was given the Spirit of Wisdom and the Spirit of Might empowering him to comprehend, gain insight and know the answers to all the questions that he was asking God.(Daniel 2:23) "**You have given me wisdom and power.** Now you have made known to me, what we asked". Daniel had "exceptional ability, with knowledge and insight, and the gift of interpreting dreams, explaining riddles and unravelling problems" (Daniel 5: 12). He was able to give the interpretations of dreams.

Wisdom is one of the seven Spirits of God mentioned in the book of Revelation. Wisdom is an excellent Spirit, who combined together with the Spirit of knowledge and the Spirit of understanding can interpret dreams, solve riddles, and explain enigmas. These Spirits and characteristics that were found in Daniel are freely available to us in our generation, given to us by our loving heavenly Father, and they are essential for our spirit, soul and body. In the book of Daniel, King Nebuchadnezzar who had had a dream was looking for someone to interpret his dream without any success, when the queen said "there is a man in your kingdom who has the Spirit of the Holy God in him; he was known in your fathers time to possess clear insight and godlike wisdom" (Daniel 5:11). The king acknowledged the fact that Daniel was wise, and that his wisdom surpassed all human capabilities, and that he had light and understanding. Later Daniel was able to understand and explain the king's dream, with this God given ability by the Spirit of understanding and wisdom.

Consider the fact that **Light,** is always portrayed together in the Bible with understanding and excellent wisdom, and we can make the connection that only God is LIGHT. The Spirit of Wisdom and Knowledge and Understanding were not only available to Daniel in times long ago; but are very much available to us in our present generation as we follow the same example and live a similar lifestyle to Daniel. This Spirit of Wisdom is available to everyone in our generation too; it all depends on the choices that we make. When we live by the principles of God we are able to get wisdom in a similar manner from God, who is the giver of all things." Every good and generous action and every perfect gift come from above, from the Father who created the lights of heaven" (James 1:17). All good things comes down from the Father of Lights who freely gives to humans all things, because we are His treasured possessions and He loves us very much; and always wants the best for us. Our choices in life may hinder this access, or process.

So who is classified as wise or a wise man? Who is considered by God to be wise?

God mentions that the wise are those who understand the will of God, and are able to redeem the time; that live life being wary and are not foolish or drunk with wine, but filled with the Holy Spirit. "But let the Holy Spirit fill you: speak to one another in Psalms and hymns and spiritual songs" (Ephesians 5:18). Singing to the Lord, these people are the ones who God classifies as 'wise'.

No one who lives a double life can receive wisdom, because one has to depart from evil, and the evil way, in order to hate, evil pride and arrogance. We desperately require the Spirit of wisdom in our present generation to assist us to keep ourselves pure and clean in a perverse world.

Wisdom- "She is a tree of Life, to those who grasp her, and those who hold fast to her are safe" (Proverbs 3:18) Wisdom can be grasped and also retained, and this can be achieved by simply studying the Bible. The preacher in the book of Ecclesiastes mentions that "Wisdom profits by giving life to those who possess her" (Ecclesiastes 7:12). Those who have wisdom are at an advantage in every aspect of life, as they have inside information easily accessible at all times.

The Spirit of Wisdom has a characteristic that is 'peaceable', and those who make peace; sow the fruit of Righteousness. Wisdom's characteristic 'peaceable', produces a fruit called Righteousness. "Peace is the seed-bed of righteousness, and the peacemakers will reap its harvest" (James 3:18). Only when a seed is sown can it grow into a tree, and God clearly refers to wisdom as a tree of 'Life', which produces a fruit called righteousness.

Those who make peace have Wisdom. This Wisdom can be found with Jesus, and it makes a person happy. On finding wisdom a person can gain understanding also, which then adds to their happiness. The Spirit of Wisdom causes a person to prosper in all that they do. Wisdom has proceeds and also brings gain and everything humans desire, and Wisdom is incomparable. The Spirit of wisdom has a voice and can speak, and be heard. We ought to listen in order to hear wisdom speak." (Proverbs 8:6) "**Listen** for **I** shall **speak** clearly (Proverbs 3:13) "Happy is he who has found wisdom, and he who has acquired understanding; for wisdom is more profitable than silver, and the gain she brings is better than gold! She is more precious than red coral, and none of your jewels can compare with her."

In order to '**get**' wisdom as the Bible tells us, we must go after her. Just like to get anything that we want in life; we endeavour to achieve it and must first make a move that gets us to the place where the thing is available. Similarly to get wisdom we must first get to the place where wisdom is available, and that only place is with God.

How does a person get to God?

The Bible informs us that we can only get to God by first approaching His Son Jesus: "No one comes to the Father except by Me" (John 14:6) is what Jesus said. When we accept Jesus in our hearts, we are sealed with the Holy Spirit, and this is when we are in the position to get the Spirit of wisdom, because at this stage we are able to unclutter our lives and rid ourselves of all that is unholy and unclean in the sight of God.

We are able to "walk circumspectly", "redeeming the time" (Ephesians 5:15-19) i.e. wary and unwilling to take risks. This sums up how we should treat our human spirits, so as not to be exposed to the traits of the enemy; we must not be drunk with wine, and must not be unwise. Our lives should be a life filled with the Spirit of God, and God centred. Only then the Spirit of wisdom can be given to us, by God and only then are we able to receive anything good.

The Spirit of wisdom and knowledge are given to us in our spirits to keep us stable, in a constantly changing world, where immorality thrives in abundance and is acknowledged by the majority of society as the normal way of life. It is extremely difficult for the person who believes in Jesus, and has accepted Him as their personal saviour, to live in the midst of all the immorality that thrives in society. And yet, we are not alone, we are not vulnerable, we are not weak; but we are strong, and we are over comers, because when we seek God with all of our hearts we are given the spirit of wisdom and the spirit of knowledge, which enhances our lives and allows us to live without and above all these sensual temptations. The Bible informs us that the Spirit of Wisdom and Knowledge are our stability and strength at all times.

"It is the Lord who bestows wisdom" (Proverbs 2:6)

"He endows the upright with ability." (Proverbs 2:7)

So wisdom is given by God, and it is sound and only reserved specifically, for the people who in God's sight are considered upright, or have a right standing with God. The spirit of wisdom gives a person the ability to achieve their goals to perfection. There follows very descriptive detailed information about the spirit of wisdom:

The Spirit of Wisdom is a loving Spirit; wisdom descends from above, and is heavenly. Wisdom is a Spirit person.

- Wisdom is pure
- Wisdom is peaceable
- Wisdom is gentle
- Wisdom is willing to yield
- Wisdom is full of mercy
- Wisdom has good fruits
- Wisdom is without partiality
- Wisdom is without hypocrisy

These above mentioned characteristics of the Spirit of wisdom are described in the book of James (3:13-18)

We have to be aware of the facts that are given in the Bible for warning, which clearly inform us that there are two types of wisdom, one of which is heavenly and the other is demonic. The characteristics of heavenly wisdom are mentioned above, and can be easily differentiated from demonic wisdom which is earthly and sensual, and is very visible in our present society; which follows the earthly sensual ways of this demonic spirit so easily. No effort whatsoever is required to follow the earthly demonic wisdom, and it is universal.

But to follow the Wisdom that belongs to God which is heavenly, takes an investment of time and effort and has to be acquired; by listening diligently to the word of God and making every effort to walk in His ways. This feels almost like swimming upstream against the tide of a river. We need to set ourselves apart from the ways of the world, not indulging in a lifestyle that contradicts God which can be challenging and difficult, but is eventually very rewarding. It is easy for people to follow the demonic spirit of wisdom of this world, because it takes no effort at all. It is like moving in the direction of the flow of a river, it is effortless and people can get carried along, but are heading towards disaster and destruction. Almost as if they would soon be swept over the rapids and be dashed; or flow into the sea and be drowned. In spiritual life this similar situation can be compared to the circumstances that surround us in our physical world. Yet most people are not even aware that alongside our physical world, exists a very real unseen spiritual world; which we also live in. It definitely does exist and has an effect on our lives according to the life we choose to live, the words we speak and the decisions we make. So it is time to wake up spiritually, since we definitely are spirit beings, and we must take our place with Jesus in the heavenly places.

Jesus does exist and He **is Wisdom**. Jesus can also take on different forms, which is explained later on. Wisdom is one of the seven Spirits of God, that Jesus is depicted holding, in His right hand, in the first chapter of the book of Revelation in the Bible. Wisdom adds ability and is the quality of being wise; and the ability to make right use of knowledge. Wisdom is learning, is skilful speculation with spiritual perception and includes sanity. The fact that Wisdom actually includes sanity makes it easy to understand why there is such an increase in mental health problems, in our society today. Although many mental health illnesses have a physical origin, there are other mental illnesses that are of spiritual origin. This can be linked with the choices that people make and don't want to acknowledge or know Jesus, and therefore their spirits are lacking the Spirit of Wisdom from God, and this is making people spiritually ill, which is manifesting physically in a mental aspect. Almost comparable to the lack of a mineral or vitamin in our physical bodies that causes a deficiency that eventually manifests as a major disease; which if left untreated would surely lead to death of the individual.

Humans do not have adequate knowledge and insight into the functioning of the brain and are therefore trying to treat or heal the problem, without the Healer. It is like trying to fix the engine of a car without reading the instruction manual of the car or knowing how the car was made or how it is going to work, but just giving it some kind of treatment that is on a trial and error basis.

"I would fill you with my spirit and make my precepts known to you" (Proverbs 1:23)

This is a cue, that we need God's Spirit to know and understand God's words, and only then can we obtain Wisdom. The need to spend more time in God's presence and more time **listening** to His Word (the Bible) is absolutely crucial and essential.

"A wise man will **hear** and will **increase** learning" (Proverbs 1:15). It is a dire necessity, an absolute essential to receive the spirit of wisdom in our spirits to be able to perceive and understand and receive instruction in our spirits from our Creator God; our heavenly Father. When we receive wisdom we are enhanced with good perception, judgement, equity, and justice. We are able to decipher the messages we are receiving from God in our spirits to make the right decisions in life. Wisdom can be taught only by God. "But as for you, the anointing which you received from Him remains with you; **you need no other teacher, but you learn all you need to know from His anointing,** which is true and no lie. Dwell in Him as He taught you to do" (1John 2:27).

Wisdom has a definite specified pathway in which there is room only for honesty. This pathway obviously leads to a specific destination which is heaven. We are sojourners in this world and the Spirit of Wisdom (the Holy Spirit, Jesus) is our companion who leads us to our heavenly abode, through this earthly journey (Proverbs 4:11) "I shall guide you in the paths of wisdom. I shall lead you in honest ways".

Wisdom can be known and perceived and received as an instruction. Wisdom is an instruction for those of us who give our very utmost attention to listening carefully to what God has to say to us each day. Wisdom gives prudence, knowledge and discretion. The earliest stage to obtaining wisdom is when one fears God or totally reverences Him (Proverbs1:7). "The fear of the lord" is the initial first stage to wisdom. So in simple explanation: Wisdom has a beginning and can be obtained by the simple process of receiving from God while also fearing God. **Wisdom** can call out, and has a loud voice and audible sound that can be maximised. We hear **her voice** in our spirits loud and clear, we feel the **vibrations** and even define them as a gut feeling, but we often permit other sounds to drown out the voice of Wisdom. We must pay attention and heed the sound of advice and instruction and direction that we receive in our spirits as tiny almost negligible electrical impulses, communication in light form that we must decode. Many a time we feel comfortable about a decision or we feel a peace in our spirit which we interpret as a comfortable feeling and we know that is the right decision; this is God communicating with us and giving us direction which we should heed. God speaks to us through His word 'the Bible'. Often it is just 'gut feelings', and sometimes it may even be an audible voice. Audible voices heard by people who have mental health problems are definitely not the voice of God.

"**Wisdom** cries aloud in the open air, **she** raises her voice in public places," (Proverbs 1:20.) The Spirit of Wisdom has emotion, because she cries. A cry could also imply a general utterance, a watchword or a battle cry; or indicate that wisdom is an official maker of proclamations. (Proverbs 8:3) "Beside the gate, at the entrance to the city, at the approach by the portals she cries aloud". There is a reason why Wisdom cries at the gates with emotion, at the entry of the city gate and at the entrance of doors of people's houses; because she knows and can see in the spirit world what our human eyes cannot see. She sees the demon spirits lying in wait in the city, on the walls, in the midst of the city, at the door of peoples' houses, in their dwellings and sends out her warning cry at places that we must not enter or go to. Wisdom can see these demon spirits lurking about, just waiting to see who they can beguile like Eve and Adam, or who they can harass or oppress or possess.

So Wisdom speaks, Wisdom has a gender "She", Wisdom has words, and Wisdom is clearly audible, which confirms that we can get wisdom by listening.

She (wisdom) has an important place of honour i.e. in the chief concourse or in an assembly of persons who take joint action together, and agree. She is also the one who accompanies us as a witness, and we can feel her reassurance in our spirits. So Wisdom can assemble and participates in the assembly of persons who have legal rights (chief concourses). Therefore **Wisdom has a legal right**.

Wisdom goes public at the openings of the gates of the city, in the assembly, at the chief concourses where people of authority meet, who agree together. The Spirit of Wisdom is present in offices of authority, and stands listening quietly to every conversation. She is willing to give excellent advice and direction, but sadly is completely ignored and not acknowledged by most people.

"Wisdom profits by giving life to those who possess her" (Ecclesiastes 7:12)

Wisdom can enter your heart (Proverbs 2:10) "For **wisdom will sink into your mind**, and knowledge will be your heart's delight".

Listen for Wisdom can be heard. Words of God can only be received by you with your permission, and your freewill and by listening to God's word. ("My son if you take my words," Proverbs 2:1)

The person, who finds **Wisdom,** also **finds happiness**. This is what every human being is looking for, but in all the wrong places. It is so simple, but yet happiness has evaded humans, or rather humans have turned away from God and still expect to be happy, and this is what makes God sad. Whereas if humans would only seek God and **listen** to **His words**; they could very easily have Wisdom and happiness absolutely free. That void in a human's soul will be filled with Wisdom, the Wisdom of God; and humans would never have to make vain effort or have a need to spend any money at all to acquire happiness that is fleeting.

The Wisdom of God is deemed more precious than the proceeds of silver or gold; and is **a permanent solution to man's problems. Wisdom can be taken hold of and can be retained.**

Wisdom is a tree of life (and trees always grow and have extremely long lives).

The Spirit of **Wisdom takes a specific pathway that is peace, and her way is pleasantness** (Proverbs 3:16-18) "In her right hand is long life; in her left are riches and honour. Her ways are pleasant ways and all her paths lead to prosperity. She is a tree of life to those who grasp her, and those who hold fast to her are safe".

"By wisdom the LORD laid the earth's foundations" (Proverbs 3:19). So wisdom was the key person present when the earth's foundations were laid. Wisdom was the architect who established earth. Wisdom **was the origin** of the earth.

Wisdom can actually depart from your eyes, if you are not careful, because wisdom has to be kept safely. We are actually instructed in our instruction manual (the Bible) about what we should do; and that is to keep "our eyes fixed on Jesus, the pioneer and perfecter of faith" (Hebrews 12:2) (Proverbs 3:21) give a clear instruction "My son . . . do **not let them out** of your sight". **Don't let them depart from your eyes.** Keep sound wisdom and discretion." Therefore we should be careful and selective in what we watch, and ensure that what we watch is not unclean or anything that can defile a person's spirit, because our eyes are one of the modes of entry into our spirit.

Wisdom can be actually acquired and retained, and this can easily be done by Listening to God's words which are the scriptures, which can be memorised and then followed carefully by living according to God's instructions and directions, which means retaining all that we have been given in the form of data, and commands (Proverbs 4:4) says "Hold fast to my words with all your heart, keep my commandments and you will have life." Get wisdom.

By retaining God's wisdom, godliness is achieved, which adds to a long life, giving a person a God like character, and making the person pious, and divine, according to God's laws (1 Timothy 4:8) "it holds out promise not only for this life but also for the life to come".

- Wisdom is the initial most important component.
- Wisdom can be exalted.
- Wisdom promotes.
- Wisdom brings honour.
- Wisdom can be embraced.
- Wisdom has accuracy.

Wisdom can deliver, has a royal delivery service as wisdom delivers a Crown.

There is a lot of action as the Spirit of Wisdom can move, there is mobility, agility and accuracy as Wisdom can place accurately or put on your head the ornament of grace that is divinely given talent or blessing, the free unmerited favour of God, that is manifested in the salvation of sinners and the bestowal of the blessings.

Wisdom can stand and she can position herself in the most appropriate place in full view at the highest level. So in any of life's situations, decisions won't be difficult or complicated because the Spirit of Wisdom can view the complete scenario of the road ahead, and will give accurate directions.

Wisdom is humble because she stands besides the way, at a common place where the paths meet; signifying the thin line between good and evil and the paths of two worlds' i.e. spiritual worlds of good and evil which exist alongside our physical world but is unseen with the human natural eye. Wisdom is described as standing on the top of the hill, as that is the most significant point. It has the best overall view, from where the complete picture is visible clearly; whereas a nearsighted view is unable to grasp the complete picture, as the view is only clear and accurate from above. So wisdom can also see afar off in the distance like a watchman from a lookout tower, and can warn you of any impending danger.

"She takes her stand at the crossroads, by the wayside, at the top of the hill;" (Proverbs 8:2)

Wisdom calls out to people, and has a voice that is specifically directed to people who are humble and willing to listen to the voice of God. A voice always involves a person, as sound produced in a larynx is uttered by the mouth as speech; it is the utterance of a guiding spirit. A call that is directed at someone attracts their attention or summons them. A voice could be a still small voice or an audible voice. It often is a powerful force of attraction or the shout of an official during a game that signifies a rule has being breached. So wisdom is also like a warning bell, which we can hear in our spirits. (Proverbs 8:4) "It is to you I call, to all mankind I appeal".

Wisdom gives instruction and advice, telling people to be cautious and wise in their conduct. Wisdom promotes caution and attention in our best interests, that is dictated by forethought and characterised by the quality of being prudent, which is wisdom applied to practice. (Proverbs 8:5) "Understand you simpletons, what it is to be shrewd, you stupid people, understand what it is to have sense".

Wisdom speaks of excellent things. Wisdom has lips, a mouth and this is the opening of any 'vessel'. When wisdom opens her lips right **things** come out making spiritual things tangible in our physical world. Indicating that if anyone has 'wisdom' dwelling on the inside them then whatever wisdom inspires the person to say, will come to pass, making it a tangible substance in a physical world. Thus bringing to pass the Biblical statement that "**faith** gives **substance to our hopes and convinces us of realities we do not see**" (Hebrews 11:1).

Wisdom has a mouth that speaks the truth and detests the devil. The Bible clarifies specifically that the devil is detested, not people. Wickedness or the wicked spirit, whose words and works are always evil: the devil is an abomination an object detestable to wisdom; (Proverbs 8:7) "for I speak nothing but the truth, and my lips detest wicked talk." Wisdom has a mouth which has words, which are with righteousness, or righteous acts and integrity. This implies that positive words are accompanied with integrity and righteous acts or actions. (Proverbs 8:8) "All that I say is right." Wisdom is words plus actions that are both righteous.

How can the devil be an abomination to the lips, or why are 'lips' mentioned in context to the devil as an abomination? Why are 'lips 'so important or given so much significance?

Lips are the edge or rim of a cavity or vessel; and therefore if lips are the opening of a vessel and truth is always spoken with the mouth, then the wicked or devil that is an abomination does not have any mode of entry into the human body, or the 'vessel'.

Entry------------lips
Vessel -----------human body

(Proverbs 8:8) "All that I say is right, not a word is twisted or crooked."

Nothing bent like a crook, deviating from rectitude or model of uprightness or righteousness, or turned aside from the truth are in the words that wisdom speaks.

(Proverbs 8:9) "All is straightforward to those with understanding; all is plain to those who have knowledge".

So wisdom is plain and easy to understand to the person who can comprehend and is fully aware and able to follow the working logical meaning, and grasps with his mind.

Proverbs 8:10 commands "Choose my instruction rather than silver, knowledge rather than pure gold". The writer is clearly telling us that the need to receive God's instruction is vital and valuable in comparison to the precious common metals; gold and silver.

Wisdom can therefore be received as an instruction or by the art of instructing or teaching. Wisdom gives information, direction, and commands, or special direction. It is enlightenment when knowledge is also received; this enhances practical skills, and enables an intimacy in relationship with our Creator spiritually, allowing us to tap into the resources of heaven.

Wisdom dwells, abides or resides, with prudence which translates as wisdom applied to practice, and attention to self interest, dictated by forethought. Wisdom has a quality of being discreet, finding out knowledge or the jurisdiction or observation by which a person is known. (Proverbs 8:12) "I am wisdom, I bestow shrewdness and show the way to knowledge and discretion."

Chapter 15

The Spirit of Understanding

The prophet Isaiah refers to the Spirit of understanding, which goes side by side with Wisdom. A person is able to clearly understand the things of God and is able to discern between good and evil, only when God gives the Spirit of Understanding to a person. The Spirit of Understanding is one of the seven Spirits of God mentioned in the book of Isaiah in the Bible. It is essential that we **'ask'** God for Understanding and Wisdom. The Bible gives us an illustration which was a reality, where Solomon was asleep and God was talking to him in his dream, and Solomon was also talking to God. And God told Solomon in his dream that he must ask God for what he wanted; and then we are told, that Solomon asked for wisdom, and God gave him, in his dream, according to his words, that he had asked. Solomon was given 'wisdom and understanding' in his dream which became a reality when he awoke.

(1Kings 3:11-12) "**Because you have asked**" . . . ."I grant your request . . . . I give you a heart so wise and so understanding";

(1 Kings 4:29) "God gave Solomon deep **Wisdom** and **insight, and understanding** as wide as the sand on the seashore, so that Solomon's wisdom surpassed that of all the men of the east and of all Egypt."

God gave Solomon exceedingly much wisdom; yet we know that Solomon was not a perfect person, he was a sinner even though he loved the Lord, because he had made a treaty with Pharaoh, and married pharaoh's daughter (they did not believe in Solomon's God because they were idol worshippers. Solomon was unequally yoked with a person who did not believe in His God.) Solomon even sacrificed and burned incense at the high places, which was clearly pagan. And yet God gave him what he had asked for; that too in his dream; only because his father, David, walked in truth and in uprightness of heart with God, and this is the reason that God showed mercy to Solomon and did not withhold from him; all that he had asked for. In fact God was pleased with Solomon's request, because Solomon did not ask for riches, and God gave it to him anyway as a bonus, along with long life.

A clear demonstration of God's love for humans is very obvious here, because Solomon loved God but at the same time was doing what he wanted to do, and yet God overlooked all that, because he knew Solomon's heart. A lot of the time, we are like Solomon and we do what we want, but God is still merciful, and gives us His Grace and loves us very much; inspite of all our shortcomings. This does not give any one of us an excuse to sin deliberately and still think that we can be categorised as followers of Christ.

The Spirit of God, Light, the Spirit of Wisdom and The Spirit of Understanding, are to be found, together.

A person who can understand is informed and has inside information which only the Holy Spirit can give to us, if we are in tune with God. Just like you have to tune a radio and then fine tune it again, before the voice on the radio can be heard clearly; even so we have to take the time to tune in, and fine tune our spirits, to hear the voice of God clearly. In order to do this, we must spend quality time with God, daily on a one to one basis, quiet time with God, not on the run. We must spend time in the 'Word' (Bible), and absorb as much information as we possibly can from the Bible in order to be saturated to the fullest.

Information is knowledge, and information enhances a deeper understanding of anything and everything. The spirit of Understanding enables us to comprehend clearly, in a more in-depth manner. Understanding makes us more aware of any situation and we are forewarned as we understand, and therefore are equipped with the ability to handle any situation however complicated it may be. It gives us the ability to act appropriately, and conduct ourselves in the most dignified, capable manner. We know that 'information is power'; which is literally true when the Bible is applied to our daily lives, as it effectively changes everything positively.

The Spirit of Understanding has the capabilities to discern good and evil and has a place of abode in a person's heart. Understanding is given by God; but before we are given anything, we are clearly instructed to **ask.**

Chapter 16

Spirit of the Fear of the Lord

God has said in (Jeremiah 32:40) "I shall put **fear** of me into their hearts, and so they will not turn away from me."

The Bible talks about two kinds of fear:

- The fear of the Lord
- The fear of man

The fear of God is godly fear, and the fear of man is demonic fear, and both these fears that are referred to in the Bible, are spirits beings.

The fear of the Lord is the **Spirit of the fear of God**. This is one of the seven Spirits of God, mentioned in the passage of scripture from (Isaiah 11:2)"a **Spirit of** knowledge and **fear of the LORD**", and also one of the seven Spirits mentioned in the book of Revelation; "the eyes which are the seven spirits of God sent to every part of the world."(Revelation5:6)

The Spirit of the fear of the Lord helps us to have an accurate perspective of life and enables us to make the right decisions in life, according to the principles of God, thus fearing God, and walking in His ways. "The first step to wisdom is the **fear** of the Lord." (Proverbs 9:10)

The fear of man is also a spirit, but it is not from God, it is a demonic spirit.

"For the spirit that God gave us is no cowardly spirit, but one to inspire power, love, and self discipline" (2 Timothy 1:7). We are not given a spirit of fear, but we are empowered with a spirit of love, power and a sound mind. The cowardly spirit mentioned is a demonic spirit of fear. Yet God's 'Spirit of the fear of the Lord', that He has put in our hearts, is so that we do not depart from Him, this Spirit has love and power and gives us a sound mind.

What is the fear of the Lord?

It is the Spirit of the fear of the Lord that empowers people to live a peaceful life that is pure and truthful.

We are given clear instructions about how to reverence God and how to live a godly life that is pleasing in His sight. "Keep your tongue from evil and your lips from telling lies" (Psalm 34:13). "Then have done with falsehood and speak the truth to each other" (Eph 4:25). Stay well clear of evil and an evil lifestyle. "Let no offensive talk pass your lips, only what is good and helpful to the occasion, so that it brings a blessing to those who hear it" (Ephesians 4:29) Speak the truth always, and don't speak harsh words. We must not cause any distress or sadness or sorrow to the Spirit of God in any manner. No corrupt communication should be allowed to proceed out of your mouth, but only good words, so that anyone hearing your words may be encouraged and strengthened (Ephesians 4:31). "Have done with all spite and bad temper, with rage, insults, and slander, with evil of any kind" (Ephesians 4:32) "Be generous to one another, tender—hearted, forgiving one another as God in Christ forgave you."

"In a word, as God's dear children, you must be like Him" (Ephesians 5:1). "Live in love" (Ephesians 5:2). Do not indulge in fornication, or anything that is spiritually unclean. We must not even participate in coarse humour or conversations that dishonour anyone. We must not make an idol of anyone or anything, and we must not be envious of anyone's possessions. "Do not seek revenge, but leave a place for divine retribution; for there is a text which reads 'Vengeance is mine, says the Lord, I will repay" (Romans 12:19). All these instructions enable us to have very clear direction for our lives.

Chapter 17

Angels

There are different categories of angels:

Mighty Angels, Angels of God or angels of the Lord or His Angels (these are the mighty angels, or the **seven Spirits of God**, referred to as the **seven stars** or the **seven eyes**, of the Lamb of God. These angels are sent out into all the earth. These angels stand in the temple of God in heaven. We do know the names of two of these angels i.e. Gabriel an archangel of greater than ordinary rank and Michael also an archangel typically represented slaying the dragon; which in anyone's opinion, is very clear that the dragon is Satan (who is not an anonymous person), because (Revelation 12:7-9) tells us, that "war broke out in heaven; Michael and his angels fought against the dragon but he was too weak and they lost their place in heaven . . . . he was thrown down to the earth, and his angels with him".

It is of extreme importance, to notice the enormous size of these mighty angels, so as to be able to comprehend in our human minds, the complexity of these Spirits of God; and how they may indwell us by the indwelling of the Holy Spirit of God.

Hosts of angels in heaven are worshipping angels, who are also ministering spirits designated to help humans on planet earth, every day of our lives. These angels are "mighty in power, which do His bidding and obey His command" (Psalm 103:20). We set the law of the spoken word in motion; by speaking God's words out aloud, by applying (speaking aloud) practically any scripture that is relevant to our lives circumstances.

Fallen angels are the demon spirits that were thrown out of heaven along with their ruler, Satan, who was also thrown out of heaven because he exalted himself before God. These fallen angels have ranks, and a hierarchy that we should be aware of. These are they who led the whole world astray (Revelation 12:9) "that ancient serpent, who led the whole world astray, whose name is the Devil, or Satan". These demonic fallen angels are still in existence on planet earth currently; but people are unaware of their presence and these demonic angels still easily lead people of the world astray because of their unawareness and ignorance in this area, and unwillingness to believe. They were originally created as angels so they know how to masquerade as 'angels of light' in order to deceive humanity,

During the life of Jesus, when He cast out a legion of demons from a man and sent them into a large herd of pigs, causing the pigs to run into the sea and be drowned; giving us an insight into the vast amount or number of demon spirits that had possessed that man and were dwelling in his spirit and body. This story is thought provoking and cautions and prompts us to evaluate ourselves and what is in our spirits, and who we permit to access our spirits. It also gives an insight into the capacity of our human spirits. (Mark 5:12-13) "The spirits begged him, 'Send us among the pigs; and let us go into them.' He gave them leave; and the **unclean spirits** came out and went into the pigs; and the herd of about **two thousand**, rushed over the edge into the lake and were drowned." All these demon spirits were inside one man and Jesus cast them out. God refers to our spirits, as vessels or containers which can contain a massive amount spiritually, depending upon what we authorise into our spirits whether it be demon spirits or whether it be God's Holy Spirit and the Spirits of God. **We have massive storage capacity in our spirits.**

Visualise the impact that a Christian can have on any situation, if we will open our mouths and make the right confessions; allowing the full force of the Spirit of God out of our vessel. It is like compressed air that is suddenly allowed to escape under very high pressure; things can be catapulted into high speed motion, accessing in an instant all that we need, through the power and might of God and His mighty angels. If only we would believe and obey instantly, when we hear the voice of God; everything would be so much clearer and would make sense to us.

We must also be aware of demon spirits and their prevailing activity, as they are masquerading as 'spirits of light', and are a counterfeit. (2 Corinthians 11:14) "**Satan himself masquerades as an angel of light**". This is why Jesus tells us that it is important to discern the spirits, so that we are not beguiled by the enemy; the devil, who prowls about seeking whom he may devour. It is absolutely essential to spend quality time with God the Father and Jesus, worshipping Him in Spirit and in truth, and spending more time studying His word, in order to gain the knowledge that is required, to be able to discern all these things. In order to do this we must set ourselves apart from the things of this world and go after the things of God.

Mighty angels are mentioned in the Bible. The seven Spirits of God that are mentioned in the book of Revelation and Isaiah are also referred to as the seven stars, which are in Jesus' right hand in the first chapter of Revelation, and Jesus explains that these seven stars are the seven angels, that are sent forth to the seven churches. These seven angels are further described in a later chapter as " .... Clothed in pure and white linen, and having their breasts girded with golden girdles" (Revelation 15:6). Jesus who stands "among the lamps was a figure like a man, in a robe that came to his feet, with a golden girdle round His breast," (Revelation 1:13). The similarities of clothing in both these verses link the "One like the Son of Man", and the seven angels that come out of the temple, as one spiritual being, who take on the form of different angels.

Jesus is this 'One like the Son of Man ', who has the seven stars or the seven angels, who are **mighty angels**, who really are the seven Spirits of God that stand before God in the temple in heaven, and these angels have a loud voice. Similarly the voice of God is described in the same manner confirming that Jesus is these seven Spirits of God, who are also seven mighty angels. Because Jesus is God He is able to be all these different personalities, and still be Jesus.

John the apostle who wrote the book of Revelation as he was instructed, recognised the angel as Jesus, and fell down to worship Him, but was told by Jesus that he must not do that because Jesus was his fellow servant, and of his brethren the prophets (Rev 22:8-9)."It was I John, who heard and saw these things. When I had heard and seen them, I prostrated myself to worship the angel who had shown them to me. But he said, 'You must not do that! I am your fellow servant with you and your brothers the prophets and with those who take to heart the words of this book" Further on in the same chapter the angel is still talking to John and says "I am coming soon, and bringing with me my recompense to repay everyone according to what he has done! I am the Alpha and the Omega, the first and the last, the beginning and the end."(Revelation 22:12). In verse 16 of the same chapter the angel is still talking to John and refers to himself as 'I' and 'Jesus', saying: "**I**

Jesus have sent my angel to you. The strong evidence confirms that this mighty angel is Jesus appearing in a different form.

"I **Jesus,** have sent **My angel** to you with this testimony for the churches" (Rev 22:16) Notice that Jesus has specific angels that He is referring to; **Jesus** also says in the same verse that He is "the Bright and Morning **Star**" So if Jesus is the STAR then He is also the **Seven Spirits of God** and the seven Angels, and only Jesus can testify. (2 Thessalonians 1:7) mentions "when the **Lord Jesus** is revealed from heaven **with His mighty angels**, in blazing fire" indicating that 'His mighty angels' are closely associated with Jesus.

Jesus often appeared in the Old Testament to various people as an angel of God and they all recognised Him, as God. For example, Manoah in the book of (Judges13: 21—22) "When Manoah realised that it had been the **angel of the LORD**, he said to his wife, 'We are doomed to die, for we have seen **God**".

All through the Bible when an angel of the Lord appeared to various people they recognised Him as God because they were simple hearted and their lives were focused on GOD, but our focus in this generation has been diverted to worldly stuff, and we have taken our eyes off Jesus. So we need to get back on track, and be ready so as to be able to recognise Jesus when He finally does come back to earth.

When the angel Gabriel appeared to Mary, and said "The **Lord is with you** . . . . Do not be afraid Mary" (Luke 1:28-30); Mary recognised him because she answered "I am the **Lord's** servant may it be to me as **you** have said." Mary, when speaking to the angel referred to him as Lord.

The **star** in the east that appeared to the wise men, that shone so brightly was actually Jesus as one of the seven Spirits of GOD guiding them. In the book of (Revelation 22:16) Jesus says "**I am** . . . . the **Bright** and Morning **star**".The bright star in the east was the guiding light, heralding the birth of Jesus on earth; and yet was Jesus himself guiding them on their way, while appearing in another form to them.

Revelation 9:1 mentions "I saw a **star** that **had** fallen from heaven to earth, and the star was given the **key** to the shaft of the abyss" Jesus came from heaven to earth and has the keys of hell.

(Numbers 24:7) "A **star** will come forth out of Jacob" and a **sceptre** from Israel, indicating that this star (Jesus) is from the lineage of Jacob (which is confirmed in the Bible); and He is this King who rules in heaven with a sceptre.

(Judges 5:20) "The **stars fought** from heaven".

(Job 38:7) "The **morning stars sang** in chorus".

(Matthew 2:2) "We observed the **rising** of **His star**".

(Matthew 2:9-10) "There before them was the **star** they had seen rising, and it **went ahead** of them until it stopped above the place where the child lay. They were overjoyed at the sight of it".

All these scriptures confirm that Jesus is this particular star that is being discussed. This star definitely is a person, because he has 'keys', He comes from (born in the lineage) of Jacob; rules with a sceptre (only kings rule with sceptres). This star fights from heaven. This star person sings, and people come to worship Him. The astrologers perceived and recognised this star, because they were overjoyed (with the Holy Spirit of God) even before they saw Jesus lying in the manger as a child. Only the Holy Spirit of God is capable of imparting this kind of exceeding great joy that causes a person to rejoice.

His star, His angels (angels of God, mighty angels), seven Spirits of God, are all different personalities but yet the same person, Jesus; who is able to transform himself into any of these characters whenever He chooses.

It is of great importance to us as spirit beings, to know and recognise Him (Jesus) in any form. We are instructed to be hospitable and also to entertain strangers; "by doing this some have **entertained angels unawares**" (Hebrews 13:2). We must persevere in doing the 'will of God' every day of our lives, no matter what the circumstances may be. In Revelation 2:26-28 God says "To him who is victorious, to him who perseveres in doing My will to the end, I will give authority over the nations . . . . I will give him the **star of dawn**" (Jesus).

The angel of God that appeared to Mary after the resurrection of Jesus, in the tomb, was also Jesus, as one of the Angels or seven Spirits of God and Mary did not recognise Him (Matthew 28:2-3) "Suddenly there was a **violent earthquake**; an **angel of the Lord** descended from heaven and came and rolled away the stone, and sat down on it. **His face shone like lightening**; his garments were white as snow". Notice that the angel has garments. When Jesus died on the Cross there was an earthquake, similarly when he rose again, there was an earthquake.

In the Bible, garments are only referred to in regard to humans, and yet this angel had 'garments as white as snow', the same description to the clothing that is referred to in the book of Revelation in which the 'One like the Son of Man (Jesus)', is described to be wearing.

Matthew 28:4 continues by saying "at the sight of Him the guards shook with fear and fell to the ground as though dead". Similarly the apostle John, when he saw Jesus as depicted in Revelation 1:17, which says "And when I saw Him I fell at His feet **as though I were dead.**" Very obviously the guards even recognised Him, as Jesus, because, like John, they too fell at His feet as though dead. In Matthew 28:5-7, the angel continues talking to the women; he obviously does not have to talk to the guards as they have already recognised him, so he says to the women "**You . . . have nothing to fear**. I know you are looking for Jesus who was crucified. He is not here; he has been raised, as he said he would be. **Come** and see the place where he was laid, and then **go quickly and tell** His disciples: "**He** has been raised from the dead and **is going ahead of you** into Galilee; **there you will see him.**" That is what I came to tell you.**" All the phrases mentioned in these scriptures; i.e. 'do not be afraid'; 'come'; 'go quickly and tell'; 'He is going before you'; 'there you will see Him'; are all Jesus' terminology and the angel was using this strategy to familiarise the women with Jesus' words so that they may recognise Him as God. He even said, **I have told you**; but they failed to recognise Him. (Matthew 28:1) "Mary of Magdala and the other Mary **came to look at the grave.**" It is clear that their mindset was that of a 'tomb' mindset as that is what they had purposed in their heart to see, the Bible clearly tells us that they 'came to see the tomb' and to change their mindset was a choice that they had to make, before they could see Jesus there or even recognise Him even though the angel was using all the terminology of Jesus. But after the angel had spoken to them they were obedient, even though they still had not recognised Jesus (Matthew 28:8-9) "so **they departed** quickly from the sepulchre **with fear and great joy** and did run to bring His disciples word. And as they went to tell His disciples, behold, Jesus met them saying Rejoice! So they came and held Him by the feet and worshipped Him."

By ruminating upon, and questioning the above verses it is possible to comprehend clearly; because it states that they went out of the tomb with 'fear and great joy'. It is understandable that when they exited the tomb they would have some sort of fear, but this 'fear' that the Bible is talking about, is accompanied with joy. So here is wisdom, Jesus was the angel and the Spirit of the fear of the lord was present there, along with the Holy spirit, whose fruit is Joy; therefore when they exited the tomb in obedience, they were accompanied by the Spirit of the fear of the Lord and the Holy Spirit (Joy), because the scripture clearly states that "they went out quickly —**with** fear and great joy". One must also notice that their obedience was instantaneous 'quick'; and because their response was instantaneous, they got an instant response from the angel, because Jesus, immediately revealed Himself to them, and said "Rejoice!" and the rest is clear that they recognised Him, and "**came and held Him by the feet and worshipped Him**".

We as spirit beings have to ensure that we have the right mind set to be able to see and perceive. To do this we have to meditate on God's words first before the transformation of our mindsets occur.

These are a few examples to illustrate that the 'angels of God or the angels of the Lord ','His Mighty angels' are the same seven Spirits of God or the seven angels or the seven stars or the seven eyes; that are mentioned in the book of Revelation and these are all '**Jesus**' in different forms; because we are clearly told in (Revelation 3:1) that **He** "has the seven Spirits of God," (Revelation 5:6) "sent to every part of the world". The key to recognising Jesus is instant obedience, which if practiced in our daily lives, will enable us to recognise Jesus and discern the times and the coming of our Lord Jesus Christ.

Chapter 18

Angels of the Lord

Angels of the Lord are recorded all throughout the Bible, and were all recognised without a doubt, by the people to whom they appeared, as God himself. The Bible also identifies these Angels as, the 'Lord'. We who are spirit beings must be observant and attentive to God so as to recognise Him. 'Angels of the Lord' are really Jesus in a different form. These angels of the Lord are described as mighty angels in the book of Revelation. (Revelation 10:1-3) "I saw another **mighty angel coming down from heaven. He was wrapped in a cloud, with a rainbow over his head; his face shone like the sun and his legs were like pillars of fire. In his hand he held a little scroll which had been opened. He planted his right foot on the sea and his left on the land, and gave a great shout like the roar of a lion; when he shouted, the seven thunders spoke**". This mighty angel is described to be enormous as he is depicted standing with one of his feet on the sea and the other on the land.

Only God is mighty in strength and Wisdom. Make note that this mighty angel came down from heaven clothed with a cloud with a rainbow upon his head, his face looked like the sun and he had feet like pillars of fire. There is a striking similarity in the description of Jesus and these mighty angels, because Jesus is capable of taking different forms. The size of this angel described is enormous because He has his right foot on the sea and his left foot on the land; he has the roar of a lion. In the Bible, Jesus is described as the "Lion from the tribe of Judah," (Revelation 5:5) the root of David. The above mentioned 'mighty angel' in the quote is a clear description of Jesus himself who roars as a lion and speaks in the voice of God as the 'seven thunders' speak, because He is God.

Revelation 1:20 clarifies that "the seven **stars** are the **angels**" (seven angels) and the "seven **lamps** are the seven **churches**". Jesus has the seven spirits of God and He has the seven stars (seven angels).

(Revelation 3:1) "These are the words of the One who has the **seven spirits of God** and the **seven stars**".

(Revelation 4:5) "Burning before the throne were **seven flaming torches**, the **seven spirits of God**".

(Revelation 5:6) "Lamb . . . He had . . . . seven eyes which are the seven spirits of God"

He (Jesus) Has:

The **Seven stars** who are the **seven angels.**

The **Seven lamps** are the **seven churches.**

The **Seven torches, seven eyes** are the **seven Spirits of God.**

When Jesus is depicted as holding the seven stars in his right hand, it means that he has the seven spirits of God and the seven angels; and when anyone is described as having a spirit in human terms we literally mean that he has a spirit within him, as it is not possible to hold a spirit in one's hand literally when one mentions the word 'has'.

So even though the apostle John saw a vision of Jesus holding the seven spirits in his right hand, the interpretation of the vision depicts that Jesus has in Him the seven spirits of God. These seven spirits of God can transform themselves into seven different forms of mighty angels and appear individually if required, and Jesus can take on the different forms of each one. Jesus is also depicted as the 'Lamb' and as the 'Lion of the tribe of Judah' (the Bible refers to Satan as trying to 'roar like a lion' in order to mimic Jesus, but really is a counterfeit who is seeking to deceive humans).

The following story of Moses depicts the actions required to recognise God, because these mighty angels are God in different form. Exodus 3:2—4 is a perfect example "an **Angel of the Lord** appeared to him as a **fire** blazing, out from a bush. Although the bush was on fire, it was not being burnt up, and Moses said to himself, 'I must **go** across and **see** this remarkable sight. Why ever does the bush not burn away? When the **LORD saw** that **Moses** had **turned aside** to **look, he called** to him out of the bush, Moses, Moses!" Verse 14 continues "and God said unto Moses "**I AM that I AM**".

God appeared to Moses in this chapter as an 'Angel of the Lord'. Note that Moses initially only 'looked' so all that he perceived in that momentary look was an Angel. A look is quite a brief action, and is not an in depth observation, or perception. But when Moses **looked** long enough or focused his attention completely, and used analytical thinking, he was now able to **behold** or perceive. This action to 'behold 'most likely provoked his thoughts, because he then decided on the action that followed simultaneously, and instantaneously, as he **said** or declared that he would **now, turn aside** or in other words temporarily put on hold what he had been occupied with doing, to focus on, and see this 'great sight', of why this bush was not burning. (Exodus 3:1) tells us that at the time Moses had been "tending the sheep," and his complete attention had been on leading the flock that belonged to his father-in-law, Jethro. So when Moses initially saw the Angel of the Lord, it was probably a fleeting glance, as his attention was swayed off the flock momentarily. Moses then made sure that the flock was safe, before turning his attention to the burning bush again; or **turning aside** so that he was now fully focused to **see** and able to perceive and fully comprehend the complete meaning of all that was happening.

Moses had a responsibility to the work that had been entrusted to him, but he was sensitive to the things of God at the same time. Moses had to initially make changes in his mind set which was programmed to 'flock tending' and align his thoughts and actions and emotions to focus on God. It was only when Moses had taken control of all these areas of his life and brought all his human emotions into complete focus and changed his mind set, that He perceived that this Spirit being, who had appeared to him as the Angel of the Lord, was actually God Himself; because Moses never asked any questions about who this angel was or what his name was, but instead he asked God what His name was, inspite of the fact that God had introduced Himself as "I AM the God of your father, the God of Abraham, the God of Isaac, and the God of Jacob" (Exodus 3:6). Moses didn't quite grasp the terminology of 'I AM' or comprehend it initially, but Moses was clearly sure that this Spirit being that he could see was God Himself, and had no doubt about it at all.

It is crucial to recognise that the Bible initially mentioned that an **Angel of the Lord** had appeared to Moses in a flame of fire, **from the midst of the bush** (Exodus3:4) states that "when the **LORD** saw that Moses had turned aside to look, **He** called to him out of the bush, 'Moses, Moses!" **God called to him out of the midst of the bush.**

Moses recognised the Angel, without a doubt, to be God, because he answered God and said 'here I am'. Moses had to **look** to **behold** and then **turn aside** to **see**; there were some human actions involved and performed before he could 'see this great sight 'of this Spirit Being in the 'flame of fire' that was not being consumed by the heat of flame and neither was the bush itself being consumed by the flames. Moses performed four physical actions:

- Look
- Behold
- Turn aside
- See

It was only after these physical actions were performed by Moses, that the Lord saw that he had gained Moses complete attention. God then spoke to Moses from the midst of the bush, knowing that Moses was now able to hear His voice and perceive. Moses was able to hear God because he was so focused.

Interestingly, while Moses was busy making his own observations, God was observing Moses, because (Exodus 3:4) says "the **Lord saw**". Similarly God is observing each one of us too, and if we declare and perform these same human actions, and God's has our attention, He will speak to us and we will be able to hear His voice, just as Moses was able to hear when he had focused his complete attention on God.

Initially Moses saw an **Angel of God**, or God appeared to Moses as an Angel of the Lord in the **midst of the bush**; and when God had Moses' complete attention, **God spoke to Moses from the midst of the bush**, and told Moses that He was God, who is called '**I AM**.' This verifies the fact that 'the Angel of God', 'God', and 'I AM' are one and the same personality, in this passage of scripture.

In like manner we as 'spirit beings' must be sensitive to the things of God, and while fulfilling all the responsibilities that we have in this life, must still find adequate time to set aside to **look**, focus our attention on God by **turning aside** from all the things in life that keep us occupied and clamour for our attention. We need to be able to **see**, to **behold** or perceive and listen to **hear**. God is observing us and watching our every move to see if we will look, glance, behold, perceive and turn aside to focus our thoughts and actions and emotions, to listen and hear and comprehend and obey His voice instantaneously. All these physical actions combined with divine interventions from God will enhance our perception and hearing, and cause us to hear His voice and differentiate it from all the many counterfeit voices in this world, and cause us to be obedient. As spirit beings it is vital to turn aside and spend time with God in His presence to be able to hear His voice and discern the spirits.

We know that there are so many voices in this world, and the Bible also confirms this in 1 Corinthians 14:10 "There are any number of different languages in the world; nowhere is without language." There are, so many kinds of voices in the world, and all of them have a different significance. Yet we are not left without divine intervention to decipher these voices, because our Creator God has made provision for those predestined. God knew us even before we were born in flesh bodies, because He knew our spirit form. (Romans 8:29) "For those whom God knew before ever they were, He also ordained to share the likeness of His Son". We are chosen to know His will and hear His voice above all the clamour and din of this world; we are empowered to recognise Him. (Acts 22:14) "the **God** of our fathers has **appointed you**, to **know His will** and **see** the Righteous One and to **hear** him **speak.**"

The Angel of the Lord appeared in a **flame of fire** to Moses. Hebrews 1:7 specifies "of the angels he says: He makes His angels winds and his ministers **flames of fire".** Revelation 2:18 mentions "the Son of God, whose **eyes flame** like **fire".** All these descriptions fit the person named Jesus (Daniel 3:22) "those who were carrying the three men were killed by the **flames;**" the **flame of the fire** killed the men that had lifted up Shadrach, Meshach and Abednego to throw them into the furnace. All these verses signify that the flame of fire 'was clearly of God, and it was supernatural. When Shadrach, Meshach and Abednego were thrown into the fiery furnace they did not get burnt but King Nebuchadnezzar saw four men walking loose in the furnace and he identified one of them to be like the Son of God (yet king Nebuchadnezzar had never seen the son of God). The fourth person i.e. the **Son of man; (Jesus)** whose eyes are described as a **'flame of fire'** burnt the men that had thrown them in.

Chapter 19

Death

We are supernatural spirit beings that live in human flesh bodies, and to return to our original state that God initially created us (in His image), which is spirit; we have to undergo some changes, like a seed or the metamorphosis of a butterfly. The apostle Paul explains it very simply as "sown a physical body, it is raised a spiritual body." (1Corinthians 15:44). We know from this scripture that there is a natural body and there is a spiritual body, confirming that man is a spirit, living in a natural physical body, which has to be shed in order to return to a spiritual form. A seed has to be first sown in the ground and die, before it can sprout into a little plant and grow, and similarly a caterpillar has to go into a cocoon and remain there without any movement before it can turn into a butterfly and fly away.

In the book of (Job 12:22) He (God) "unveils mysteries deep in obscurity and into thick darkness he brings light." The shadow of death is brought out into the light.

It is important to notice that 'death' is a shadow, and to have a shadow there must be an object or a person that is standing in front of the light to enable a formation of a shadow.

The Psalmist refers to the "valley of the shadow of death" in (Psalm 23:4); really he is referring to Satan's shadow in the valley.

In (Job 28:22) it is written "Destruction and Death declare, 'we know of it only by hearsay." **Destruction** and **Death** the two demon spirits speak and **say,** that they have **heard** with their **ears**. In this scripture it is very clear that there are two people talking as the word 'say' indicates, and that these two people can hear as their 'ears' have been mentioned. These two people or persons are spirit beings. In this scenario, Destruction and Death are distinctly persons; because they are talking. So the names of these two persons are Destruction and Death, and they are talking and speaking (so must have a mouth and a tongue) and can hear, and have ears. It is apparent to see that ears are the anatomical structures or body parts of a person, so Destruction and Death are clearly evil spirit persons talking, saying and hearing. Destruction and Death are having a discussion, a conversation. So this 'shadow of death 'talked about is the evil or demon spirit named 'Death' who is really 'Satan' standing in the' light', or in-between us and God, creating a shadow. Jesus brings this shadow of death to light: "light has dawned on those who lived in the land of death's dark shadow." (Matthew 4:16) What happens when shadows are put into the light? The answer is that they disappear, or are dispelled.

So death, which most people are afraid of, is only a shadow of the devil; it is not even real and does not have any substance and cannot harm us in any way if we are walking with Jesus in the light; because death is a shadow. Shadows are non-existent and harmless images that are counterfeit. Bodily death or the transition phase of the spirit is not to be feared; but the death of the spirit is to be feared as that is the demonic realm of Death and Destruction. This is why God tells us to 'choose life', so that when we are in Jesus, our spirits will live on and have eternal life. Death that every human is fearful of is only a transition phase of our body, shedding an earth suit, to be raised a spiritual being; or the release of the spirit man from his 'earth suit'; the 'human body'. The procedure of the earth suit dying may be painful during the process of shedding it, but death cannot kill a spirit or the spirit of a person that is in Jesus, because Jesus conquered 'Death', and also has the keys to the locations or areas designated for Death and Destruction, which is called 'hell', so that they cannot take God's children there.

The devil's shadow is a counterfeit image of him, which is powerless as it is only a shadow and has no substance at all; unlike God's image that has power, substance and is tangible and very real i.e. **'humans.'**

Chapter 20

Demon spirits

As spiritual beings, it is of utmost importance that we have awareness about these lying, conniving, deceiving counterfeit spirits who exist in the earth's atmosphere. They love to latch on to human spirits causing depression, oppression and possession, if we will allow them either in ignorance or by an individual's choice. It is important to be able to discern and recognise these demon spirits who can take various forms with ease, and deceive humans. The Bible tells us to discern the spirits. These spiritual demons are everywhere in our spirit realm, but only for a period of time; until the return of Jesus Christ to the earth; when they will be cast into the lake of fire, for which they are destined. The eternal fires of hell were created for the devil and his demon angels, and were not created for man at all; and man has a choice, but the devil knows that his time is very limited, and therefore he tries his best to drag every soul that he can deceive with him to hell. (Revelation 12:12) "Woe to you, earth and sea, for the Devil has come down to you in great fury, knowing that his time is short!" So being ignorant is extremely dangerous for one's soul.

These demon spirits have rank and a hierarchy and even have a king over them. (Revelation 9:18) "Their king . . . . the angel of the abyss, whose name in Hebrew is Abaddon . . . . the Destroyer". Demon spirits can perform great signs and speak great things, and blasphemy. We must be extremely aware of their capabilities and tactics so as not to be fooled by them in any manner. Revelation 16:14 "These are demonic spirits with power to work miracles". They have the ability to take different forms and make appearances. We need God's Holy Spirit to help us to identify and spot them by their characteristics and behaviour, especially when they take possession of the soul of a person. Always be alert and on guard spiritually; do not to be enticed or conned by these crafty creatures. These spirits have names and are designated to physical locations on earth; as revealed to us in the Bible in Psalm 55 and also in other scriptures. The Psalmist names the demon spirits giving the locations of some of them. The name of each demon indicates their job description. Some of the names of these demon spirits are as follows:

- **Sin** is a demon crouching at the door (Genesis 4:7).
- **Death** (Psalm 55:4) (Revelation 6:8) "Rider's name was Death".
- **Hades** (Revelation 6:8) "Hades followed close behind".
- **Fear** (Psalm 55:5).
- **Trembling** (Psalm 55:5).
- **Raging wind** (Psalm 55:8).
- **Tempest** (Psalm 55:8).
- **Violence** (Jeremiah 6:7).
- **Strife** . . . . **in the city and on its walls** (Psalm 55:9-10).
- **Mischief** (Psalm 55:10).
- **Trouble/sorrow** (Psalm 55:10).
- **Sorrow/"trouble and Mischief"** . . . . are in the **midst of the city** (Psalm 55:10).
- **Destruction** . . . . is rife with it": in its **midst.** (Psalm 55:11).
- **Oppression** (Psalm 55:11).
- **Deceit** (Psalm 55:11).
- **Blood thirsty** (Psalm 55:23).
- **Treacherous** (Deceitful) (Psalm 55:23).
- **Wickedness** (Psalm 55:15).

"Its **public square** is never free from **oppression** and **deceit**." **Deceit** and **guile** are ever present and never depart from the **streets.** They are also in the **public squares** (Psalm 55:11).

Wickedness—is **in their homes and dwells among them;** "their homes are haunts of evil." (Psalm 55:15).

"**Violence** and **outrage** echo in her **streets**;" spoil is heard **in the city** (Jeremiah 6:7).

Psalm 55:3 informs us about the **voice of the enemy**, which are "hostile shouts", or "the shrill clamour of the wicked". The enemy definitely has a voice. They have wings too. Their wings make a sound "like the noise of many horses and chariots charging into battle" (Revelation 9:9).

Other humans on planet earth are not our enemies, whatever their colour or religion or status in life maybe. These demon spirits are the enemy of mankind that are causing havoc on planet earth.

These demon spirits can be heard audibly. (Psalm 55:9) "frustrate and divide their counsels, Lord! I have seen violence and strife in the city"; which confirms to us that demons have tongues, and take counsel together. "These demons stand behind every idol we create in our lives; to receive the worship of humans. An idol is anything that we give our attention to and desire and prioritise other than God. These demons also speak flattery and vain things, their conversations are always full of vanity. "For the household gods utter empty promise" (Zechariah 10:2). Humans need to beware because the enemy (Satan) has a voice. We need to learn to discern the voice of God and recognise the voice of God; so as not to be deceived by the enemy's voice.

Recognising these spirits is like being forewarned and thus forearmed, enabling us to use our authority in Jesus name effectively, to diffuse their activity and foil their plans; by commanding them directly (using their specific names), to go away from you or your loved ones. Their names very clearly describe their demonic characteristics and activity and give us an insight into their demonic hierarchy, and its functioning. Demon spirits are described to have faces. (Revelation 9:7) "Their **faces were like human faces** and their hair like women's hair; they had teeth like lions teeth".

An awareness and acknowledgement of the existence of this demonic activity in our spirit realm is of utmost importance in our daily walk with Jesus, as it enables us to use the power invested in us by God's Holy Spirit, to speak and command our successful futures into existence or reality. No demon spirit can sabotage our future or destiny because we then have authority in Jesus name using His words to create a way, where there is no way. No demon spirit can stand up to the name of Jesus or come against anything commanded in His name, because the Bible clearly specifies that everything in heaven and on earth and under the earth, must bow to the name of Jesus.

The Bible also informs us that when the enemy comes against us in life's situations; almost like a flood, then the Holy Spirit will protect us and shield us from all evil. "His glory will come in like a swift river on which the wind of the lord moves" (Isaiah 59:19). The Holy Spirit raises the military or ceremonial flag in the spirit realm that celebrates victory to remind the devil that the battle is the Lord's, and the victory has already been won when Jesus conquered death and "led captivity captive" (Ephesians 4:8). The demon spirits named 'Sin', 'Death', and 'Captivity' were conquered when Jesus died and descended into hell before ascending into heaven. That is how Jesus was able to lead the demon spirit 'Captivity', captive. Demons can trick and deceive human spirits, but they cannot take human spirits captive, because Jesus has imprisoned or taken captive the demon spirit named 'Captivity' and has completely disarmed him; so that he is out of action. Ignorance about demon spirits and demonic activity, allows the devil and his cohorts to wreck havoc in the lives of humans. Demons can take possession of human spirits, but are unable to keep them captive.

During Jesus' life here on earth as a man (which no man can deny because our international calendar each year acknowledge the dates being set to 'Anno Domini—A.D.-in the year of our Lord, and B.C.-before Christ.) Jesus often rebuked demon spirits and even asked them their names, and healed people sometimes, by commanding the demon spirits by their names, to leave the person's body.

People unknowingly permit demon spirits to wreck havoc in their lives by committing works that are contradictory to the works of Jesus, and become workers of these demon spirits without even being aware of the facts or knowing it. Ignorance is dangerous (Psalm 5:5) "you hate all evil doers". God hates all the workers of the demon spirit named iniquity.

(Proverbs 10:29) "But he brings destruction on evildoers". The demon named Destruction will come to people who work for the demon spirit named Iniquity.

We imagine Satan to be a very ugly creature who has no intelligence whatsoever; but he was originally a very beautiful, intelligent spirit being, and he still is a very intelligent being; which is why he is able to deceive people so easily. Satan was in Eden, the garden of God, and he was an anointed cherub on the Holy mountain of God. Satan was perfect until iniquity was found in him, when his heart was lifted up and he became proud because of his beauty. Brightness was one of his features, which is why he can masquerade as an angel of light and convince people. Satan's wisdom was corrupted and he wanted to be God and wanted all the praise and worship for himself. He purposed in his heart to exalt himself above God because of which God cast him out of heaven to the earth. (Ezekiel 28:13) "You (Satan) set the seal on perfection; you were full of wisdom and flawless in beauty. In an Eden, a garden of God you dwelt; adorned with gems of every kind". (Ezekiel 28:17) "Your beauty made you arrogant; you debased your wisdom to enhance your splendour. I flung you to the ground . . . ."

Satan is able to transform himself as an apostle of Christ, and also as an angel of light; his demon spirits who possess and indwell people, are also able to transform themselves as ministers of righteousness, and thus deceive people. This is why we must be alert, on our guard and well informed in the Word of God; so as not to be fooled by these lying spirits, who are everywhere. (2 Corinthians 11:13-15) "Such people are sham apostles, confidence tricksters masquerading as apostles of Christ. And no wonder! Satan himself masquerades as an angel of light, so it is easy enough for his agents to masquerade as agents of good. But their fate will match their deeds".

The good news is that Satan and these demon spirits do not understand the language of God which is 'tongues', and if one communicates with God in tongues, which is a special language given to a person by the Holy Spirit of God, then that is our hot line to the Creator which the demons cannot tamper with. (Zephaniah 3:9) "Then I shall restore pure lips to all peoples". (Matthew 10:20) "It will not be you speaking but the Spirit of your Father speaking in you". Demon spirits do not have physical bodies but are always seeking human bodies, so that they can have access to their souls by means of deception. As spiritual beings we must always be on our guard and be fully aware of all the tactics of these demon spirits, who are really fallen angels; whose only aim is to deceive people and possess their souls and control them till they are destroyed completely.

Chapter 21

Spiritual Creatures of Light

We are spiritual creatures in shining armour, because we are creatures of Light, and God is our Father. Interestingly, lights always have a power supply.

James 1:17-18 directs our attention to the light source, "**Father** who created the **lights** of heaven. With Him there is no variation, no play of passing shadows. Of **His** own choice He brought us to birth by the word of truth to be a **kind** of first fruits of **His creation**."

God is Light and He is the Father of Lights. We are these 'lights' of whom God is the Father, because Jesus said that we are lights that shine in the darkness. It is clear that we humans are of His kind. We are His creatures created in Christ Jesus for good works.

We do however, have a spiritual enemy to combat whether we are aware of it or not, and being ignorant about it does not benefit us in any manner, because humans are constantly being attacked, physically in health and also spiritually in soul. This calls for spiritual warfare, and the apostle Paul informs us "For our struggle is not against human foes, but against cosmic powers, against the authorities and potentates of this dark age, against the superhuman forces of evil in the heavenly realms" (Ephesians 6:12). We have to wrestle against a hierarchy of demon spirits who are fallen angels; principalities and powers and against spiritual wickedness in high places, not against flesh and blood.

Knowing who your spiritual enemy is matters most of all, and is of utmost importance. Our adversary is the devil who walks about like a roaring lion, seeking whom he may devour. The devil walks and seeks and roars or tries to roar like a lion, but actually he is not a lion. So the devil is a spirit person or being who walks, and therefore to walk he must have legs; he also seeks, so to seek he must surely have a brain and eyes, and to roar he must have a mouth too; this gives us a visual imaginary picture of a spirit person and the Bible warns us that this spirit person is our adversary.

The Devil has a limited amount of time on planet earth, before the return of Jesus to earth, and he knows that this is all the time that he has got before he is thrown into the lake of fire which is prepared for him. So he is using his intelligence to create havoc on earth and cause as much calamity as possible. While man is busy blaming God for all the wars, hunger, famine, and calamities; Satan is taking advantage of man's ignorance and tricking humans, and taking as many souls as he possibly can to hell. In the meantime man is blaming God and questioning God's credentials and saying that if there is a God, and He is a God of love, why is he allowing and causing all the suffering in the world? The Bible clearly states that "every good and generous action and every perfect gift come from above, from the father who created the lights of heaven." (James 1:17). Satan is the "commander of the spiritual powers of the air," (Ephesians 2:2) for a limited time, so really we need to be blaming the devil for all the suffering in this world, because he has deceived humans all this time.

Put on your spiritual armour "take up the armour of God," (Ephesians 6:13) is a command and a red alert that must not be ignored, so as to be able to withstand the evil tactics of the devil, and to triumph. We are more than conquerors only in Christ Jesus.

Chapter 22

Watchers

An awareness of demonic presence and activity in this world should not bother us or frighten us in any way because Satan has already lost the battle with Jesus; and Jesus has victory over him and all his demon cohorts. When we accept Jesus in our hearts; we too are victors over the enemy, and need not let anything worry us anymore. But we must be alert and vigilant to the strategy of the evil ones, and always prepared for spiritual battle dressed in our spiritual armour at all times just like soldiers on the front lines, we must eat and sleep in our armour, and always speak the words of God written in the Bible which have power over all the power of the enemy.

The Word of God is the sword of the spirit, which we must be ready to wield instantly when required. To be able to do this we must be diligent to spend time meditating on His word, so that it can sink down into our spirits, like the safe deposit vaults of a bank where we can put our money in, and when we require it we have plenty to withdraw.

King Nebuchadnezzar had a dream, which God revealed to Daniel, and in that dream the king saw "a great image" (Daniel 2:31). Its feet were partly of iron and partly of clay. "Iron does not mix with clay" (Daniel 2:43).Clay represents human beings, and iron represents the demonic spirits. This indicates, that in the end times, demon spirits (they) will mingle or try to mingle with the seed of men or the offspring of men.

But we need not fear or be afraid of anything because there are spiritual 'watchers' (Daniel 4:13)" a watcher a holy one coming down from heaven". "This issue has been determined by the watchers and the sentence pronounced by the holy ones. 'Thereby the living will know that the Most High is sovereign in the kingdom of men" (Daniel 4:17). These are 'watchers' who make a decision by their decree, and only God has the authority to make decrees; therefore this watcher is Jesus in the form of a 'watcher', who is also the 'holy ones' who are also the seven spirits of God sent out into all the earth. This confirms to mortals that it is ultimately God who still rules in this world, and can overrule any decision made by man.

We also have divine help and intervention available to us. Michael the great prince (Daniel 12:1) "Michael the great captain who stands guarding your fellow countrymen; and there will be a period of anguish such as has never been known ever since they became a nation till that moment. But at that time your people will be delivered, everyone whose name is entered in the book". (Daniel 9:25) Messiah is the "one anointed, a Prince," Michael is a watcher over people. Michael is also one of the seven Spirits of God i.e. the Spirit of Might who is also Jesus. Michael is Jesus because everyone whose names are found written in the book is delivered, and the Messiah is the Prince. Michael is also one of the Angels of God.

We have the mighty armies of Heaven backing us, at all times, so we need not be afraid. "The Most High is sovereign over the realm of humanity". God rules in the kingdom of men; the Heavens do rule; "He does as he pleases with the host of heaven, and with those who dwell on earth" (Daniel 4:25-35).

Chapter 23

Hot Line Communication

We are seated with Christ in heavenly places (Ephesians 2:6) "and He raised us up in union with Christ Jesus and enthroned us with Him in the heavenly realms". (Luke 11:2) "Your kingdom come", your will be done on earth as it is in heaven. Biblical statements confirm that whatever happens in heaven, the same happens here on earth in our dimensional world.

This confirms the fact that when we give our lives to Jesus and make a declaration of it with our mouths, something happens in our universe. Our words have a mechanical, electrical energy that is released, causing complex mathematical changes in the universe and linking us directly to the throne room of Heaven. This makes the invisible power line live, with energy flowing directly from the throne of God in a flash when we declare anything in the name of Jesus; especially while using Jesus' own words and terminology.

The fact that we are spirit beings connected to a higher source in the spiritual world, who is God, can be explained. The words we declare with our mouths create the existence of things in our world and shape our future. Words spoken in the physical realm have power in the spiritual realm. Even though they are invisible they create energy in the unseen world, and we know this by the practical way in which radio frequencies can pick up these signals or words and transmit them to another location almost instantly.

Revelation 4:3 informs us that John saw in his vision the throne room of heaven, and a "**rainbow** around the throne in appearance like an **emerald;** before the throne there was a sea of glass like **crystal**". We know from the scriptures that God is light and dwells in unapproachable light. Jesus said "I am the light of the world" (John 8:12), and then he also told us "you are light for all the world" (Matthew 5:14).

Understanding the complexity of the phenomenon of the 'emerald'; that John saw in the throne room of heaven, and the presence of the 'sea of glass: like crystal'; all have to do with the refraction of light. It is well known that Emeralds are precious stones which are different shades of green or colourless; can be used as beacons, have a refractive index and birefringence characteristics. The splitting of the ray of light into two rays; sounds familiar, the 'greater light to rule the day' and the 'lesser light to rule the night'. The emerald being the beacon light refracting the rays of light emanating from God Himself; the crystals also contributing to the refraction of light, and sound, the communication system. It is evident that everything in our universe works on light, and the Biblical evidence states that the first thing that God spoke into being was light; because He is Light.

Created in the image of God, we are light, and that is how the Creator of the universe communicates with us in our spirits; by light, and sound waves in words from the Bible; and through the Holy Spirit of God with our very soul, which is the seat of all our emotions. When we pray we are heard immediately by God the Father. Our unbelief may stall the answer from coming through instantly, or prevent us from hearing the answer. "He who asks must ask in faith, with never a doubt in his mind; for the doubter is like a wave of the sea tossed hither and thither by the wind. A man like that should not think he will receive anything from the Lord" (James 1:6-7).Child like faith is so important to make receiving easy when we talk to God.

The need to maintain excellent communication with our creator God is absolutely essential and crucial. Without a communication line we are definitely doomed to peril and destruction. Communicating with God is extremely simple and easy, as we can talk to God just like we talk to any other human being. It is the listening that takes some training and practice, but is easily achievable as the Holy Spirit of God is there to assist us and guide us.

We initially have to set apart time each day which is undisturbed and uninterrupted in a private location from everyone else. This must be something we do because we want to spend time with God; it must be a desire to seek Him. A secret place is ideal, as it is quiet, unseen and hidden from the world; undisturbed by any circumstances, a place where you spend special private time with God. When we set ourselves apart from the world it is easy to connect with God on a one to one basis. We must shut out the clamour and din of our world, and connect with God by being in His presence and worshipping Him. Sometimes just sitting quietly and focusing our thoughts on Jesus is a greater benefit, as we begin to hear more and learn more from God. By mentally shutting out all unnecessary thoughts and thinking about the words of God and saying them aloud we are able to secretly connect to GOD, our heavenly Father, spiritually. We somehow then enter another dimension as we focus on Jesus, as He is the 'door'.

What God gives us spiritually in this other dimension in the format of His Words as we connect, will manifest in the dimension of our physical world, when we confess it (speak God's words aloud). Our secret meetings with God each day is rewarded by Him publicly for all to see when He blesses us in our physical world as a result, in health, strength, wealth, peace and joy. (Matthew 6:6) "When you pray, go into a room by yourself, shut the door, and pray to your father who is in secret; and your Father who sees what is done in secret will reward you. In your prayers do not go babbling on . . . ."

Chapter 24

Life with Jesus

Come to Jesus, great and small,

He is the answer for us all,

He is fun to be around,

Especially when you're run aground.

When you're sad and full of gloom,

He says 'Cheer up! I'm coming soon!

He has peace and joy to give,

He died that you and I might live,

Eternal life forever more,

And Jesus is the only door!

His blood was shed for you and me,

To cleanse our sin and set us free.

So do not tarry, do not wait,

Or you my friend, might be too late.

Ask Him into your heart, **right now**.

It is the perfect time to plough.

Don't dismay and don't look back,

O Perfect day! He's coming back!

He's coming back in all His glory,

We'll reign with Him, and that's another story!

Chapter 25

My Mountain Valley

Jesus is surely coming back to take us with him; so our mortal bodies will be transformed in the twinkling of an eye when the trumpet sounds and the Lord appears in the clouds when every eye on earth will see Him. The prophet Zechariah informs, alerting us that "a day is coming of the Lord" ; "His feet shall stand on the Mount of Olives", "and the Mount will be cleft in two by an immense valley running east and west". Then you will escape through My mountain valley. "On that day, whether in summer or in winter," (Zechariah 14:1-9) The time factor of God's return being summer and winter could possibly be explained; that, it will be summer on one continent while it is winter on another continent at the time of His return.

So there is a mountain valley where there is safety for God's people, and it is secure because it is in the shadow of the Almighty. His feet are on the Mount of Olives, which will split, creating a huge valley of solid rock consisting of pure sheer mountainside; which the Lord refers to as 'My mountain valley', because God is standing here with His feet on the mountain which has just split. So it is safe because we are in the shadow of the Almighty. Which is unlike the "valley of the shadow of death" (Psalm 23:4), which is a valley where the demonic spirit named 'death' is standing and casting a shadow, and it is unsafe in this valley, and frightening, dreadful and horrible.

Chapter 26

Spiritual Vision

Put on your spiritual spectacles by aligning your life with the righteousness of God, and turning away from the things of the world that hold our attention or clamour for priority; and your spiritual vision will clear up, and have perspective, and not have blurred vision anymore. Spiritual vision is a necessity for our spirit person.

Jesus can take many different forms and appear in many different ways to humans, and has done so throughout the centuries, and some recognised Him and some did not. Some training is required to recognise Jesus when He comes again, and returns to planet earth. At creation Jesus was present as "the Spirit of God hovered over the surface of the waters" (Genesis 1:2), and God spoke the world into existence. God appeared to Abraham by the terebinth trees of Mamre as 'three men' and Abraham recognised God, and called Him "My Lord" (Genesis 18:30). God appeared to Jacob in a dream. "In a dream he saw a ladder, which rested on the ground with its top reaching to the heaven, and angels of God were going up and down on it."(Genesis 28:12). Clearly it is stated that this ladder was set up; so obviously it is still in existence because the Bible does not mention anywhere that it was taken down, so it is still set up. The secret is that we need to '**dream and behold**', to be able to see spiritually.

God led the children of Israel through the desert, and "the **Lord** went before them by day in a **pillar of a cloud** to lead them the way; and by night in a **pillar of fire,** to give them light; to go by day and night"

(Exodus 13:21).The pillar of fire was also their protection. Does the word 'cloud 'sound familiar in regards to Jesus, who ascended to heaven in a cloud and then will appear again in a cloud; or does the word 'fire' sound familiar, the flame of 'fire' that burned the men that threw Shadrach, Meshach and Abednego into the furnace or the eyes of Jesus described as a flame of fire, in the first chapter of Revelation? All these statements and words refer to Jesus.

In (Exodus 23:20) God declares "Behold I send an **Angel** before thee to keep thee in the way and to bring thee into the place which I have prepared. Beware of **Him,** and **obey His voice** and provoke Him not, for He will not pardon your transgressions: for **My name is in Him**".

In the New Testament (Mark 16:1, 5, 9, 12, 14) Mary Magdalene, Mary the mother of James and Salome came to the tomb on the first day of the week.

"They went into the tomb, where they saw a young man sitting on the right hand side, wearing a white robe"

"He appeared first to Mary Magdalene; out of whom He had cast seven demons."

"After that **He appeared in another form** to two of them as they walked and went into another country."

"Still **later He appeared** to the eleven while they sat at the table."

Jesus first appeared as a 'young man', then after that he took 'another form 'and appeared to the two disciples, who ran and told the other disciples who would not believe them. Then **He appeared for the third time in the form that was recognisable** or similar to how he was before being crucified, because the eleven disciples recognised Him immediately all together. This is because they had sat at a table with Him before His crucifixion and therefore it was a repetitive situation which they had been familiar with. This demonstrates the fact that **Jesus can appear to different people in different forms, or he can take on different forms when He makes an appearance**, and if we are not filled with the Spirit of God, we will not be able to recognise Him.

On the contrary if we are filled with the Spirit of God we will be able to distinguish His voice and hear Him, and recognise Him. We must beware of 'Unbelief', or the demon spirit named 'unbelief' which can spiritually blind a person temporarily; Jesus had to rebuke the 'unbelief' in His disciples before they could recognise Him. Only persons or people are rebuked when they do something wrong, in this instance it was the demon spirit causing the disciples to be momentarily blinded so the demon had to be rebuked, before they could recognise Him.

Jesus appeared first to Mary Magdalene inside the tomb as a young man who was wearing a long white robe. This was clothing that Mary had seen Jesus wear; she was used to seeing Him dressed in such type of clothing. Mary recognised Him because she had the Spirit of the Fear of the Lord living on the inside of her—who is the revealer of secrets (Psalm 25:14) "the Lord confides his purposes to those who fear him". God reveals His secrets from the Bible to those who fear Him, and also gives them revelation knowledge to understand things better in life's situations. Jesus had cast out seven demon spirits in the past from Mary and then filled her with the seven spirits of God, one of which is 'the Spirit of the Fear of the Lord', and this is why Mary had no trouble recognising this 'man sitting in the tomb' to be Jesus. We too as spirit beings need to be filled with the Seven Spirits of God to be empowered to recognise Jesus in any form in which He may appear to us; and to live life in the Spirit to the fullest, knowing the things of God and obeying His voice.

Chapter 27

Words are Keys

The key to victorious living is the declaration we make when we speak God's words or practically apply the scriptures in the Bible that describe the outcome we desire; these are the solutions to problems that each one of us face in life. God's words are power packed, and when we begin to declare these words in faith over our situations we speak into the spirit world and are able to draw out from the spirit realm things that God has placed there for us, that are just waiting for us to call out.

There is some action required on our part before we can see the manifestation of this spiritual principle, and the instruction that we are given by GOD to do this, is first of all to have unity and speak in unity, and this instruction is hidden in the book of (Genesis 11:6), where God is speaking and says "as **one people** with a **single language**, and now they have started to do this; from now on **nothing they have a mind to do will be beyond their reach.**" The people were building a tower to reach the heavens, which was not in God's plan, and God saw them and said the above mentioned statement, and God then confused their languages and made them speak in different languages so that they could not understand each other. And yet here is a key, speech in unity, which if applied, works perfectly. This is the same principle in Matthew 18:19 where Jesus said, "If two of you agree on earth about any request you have to make, that request will be granted by My heavenly Father"; and when He said that we must call **the things that are not in existence in our physical world, as though they were existent.** This requires faith to be able to believe God, and take Him at His word,

175

and speak His words over our life's situations, even when everything is looking bleak, such as a doctors' negative report.

Our faith, manifested in our spoken words, using God's words, can turn situations around miraculously; even though it may take time to manifest in the natural, the process is set in motion. Just like seeds of grain, sown in the ground, that take time to grow before they can be harvested, there is a similar time span before we can harvest the crop of our words. The words we speak today decide our future, and this is why we are told to guard your heart, for out of it flow the issues of life. So whether you speak in ignorance and declare negative words, or whether you speak knowingly and declare positive God given words, you will have a harvest of your words in due season.

We must declare as the Psalmist said "LORD, set a guard on my mouth; keep watch at the door of my lips" (Psalm 141:3). Satan does not have any material to work with to disrupt our lives, other than the negative words that we speak in whatever situation we are going through. If we cut off his supply of negative words spoken by humans we can turn every situation around for the good in our lives. God's words unlock the supernatural realm and become a reality in our natural physical world. Similarly negative words work in a similar manner. Never even declare negative facts, however much they are staring you in the face in reality, we must become fools for Christ and declare God's positive words in the most negative situations and God is faithful to bring to pass all that we say in faith, believing, without any doubt or unbelief.

Just because your children may have strayed from the path that leads to life and have got side tracked by the temptations in the world, does not mean that you give up on them or that they are lost forever. Never give up, but begin to command your situation and speak over your children's lives positively. Because the Lord says "**I shall make My words a fire in your mouth**" (Jeremiah 5:14) "**I shall deliver you (put your child's name) from the clutches of the wicked, I shall rescue you from the grasp of the ruthless.**" (Jeremiah 15:21) "**Your children will all be instructed by the Lord, and they will enjoy great prosperity**" (Isaiah 54:13). "**I shall contend with all who contend against you and deliver your children from them.**" (Isaiah 49:25). Release the power of God; over your child and bring them back: by constantly confessing God's words over their lives. **God's words have power and they are life; "He himself delivered them**" (Isaiah 63:9).

"The tongue has power of life and death;" (Proverbs 18:21); your tongue has this power whether you acknowledge it or not. Keep up this confession of God's words daily. Words in action are works of faith, and it allows God to work in your situation to turn it around positively. The Lord promises us that "the wicked will never again overrun you; they are totally destroyed" (Nahum 1:15). Each one of God's children has divine protection, and we must declare it aloud so that the angels can go to work on it. "Have no fear; stand firm and see the deliverance that the LORD will bring you this day" (Exodus 14:13).

Jesus is the Door to the supernatural world of Heaven and he said "Behold I have set before you an open door" (Revelation 3:8). The ladder is still set up from earth to heaven; where the door is, note this is the same ladder that Jacob dreamed about where the Angels he saw were ascending and descending on it; this ladder is a one way access currently; indicating that it is not for us to climb into heaven at the moment in our physical state but it is to access spiritual intervention from heaven itself that comes down to us, to aid us supernaturally. We need to visualise every situation positively, and dream dreams and have visions, and then speak them into existence by the power invested in us by our Creator himself; and use the power of His words spoken over our life's situations to change our world and make all things good.

As spirit beings in communion with God we have the spiritual authority to speak and command our situations in life. We are anointed with the Holy Spirit of God, as we are one with Him and the Bible confirms that God speaks through us; "It will not be you speaking, but the Spirit of your Father speaking in you" (Matthew 10:20).

Chapter 28

God's Love

God loves each one of you out there,
Whatever your burden, whatever your care,
He's with you every step of the way,
To make your path shine bright as day.
Do not dismay, God loves you! Dear,
And says that He is always near.
Cheer up! My friend, there's more to life,
Than moping around, because of strife.
Throw off the gloom.
He's coming soon!
There's work for us, we must desire,
Lost souls to rescue from hell's fire!
Chin up! My friends 'God loves each one,
All must be saved by His dear Son!

Chapter 29

You are Special

We have nothing to fear in the days ahead, if we are walking with the Lord Jesus Christ, because we are reassured in the Bible that our "God will supply all your needs out of the magnificence of his riches in Christ Jesus" (Philippians 4:19). The fact that you are reading this book is no coincidence; you were destined to read it. It is a "God-incidence", and God loves you very much; you are His most treasured possession. You are the only one of a kind on planet earth who has your finger prints. You are unique, God's masterpiece, wonderfully made, by the Master of the Universe Himself. There is no other you. You are special and dearly loved by God, no matter who you are or what you've done or where you have been. Jesus loves you just the way you are, "For **God so loved the world that he gave His only Son**, that **everyone** who has faith in Him may not perish but have eternal life" (John 3:16).

Our God who is the "High and exalted One" (Isaiah 57:15), who is of great size, stature, great intensity, is great in rank, status and importance; is noble, remarkable, and of imposing height, around whom the whole universe revolves.

"I dwell in a high and holy place and with him who is broken and humble in spirit, to revive the spirit of the humble, to revive the courage of the broken" (Isaiah 57:15). This great big mighty God loves us so much and lives in us when we invite Him into our lives. He lives in or occupies eternity, has a name 'Holy' and yet dwells or formally lives and remains in a specified place in our spirits with humans (only those who recognise that they have done wrong, have feelings of remorse, are repentant, and ask Jesus into their lives). This great God dwells with humans to revive human spirits and human hearts (soul). God loves the souls which He has made and does not want their spirits to die. If there is no repentance and remorse the soul is unclean and the spirit can die. All we need to do is to obey His voice only and do accordingly as instructed. "GOD'S divine power has bestowed on us everything that makes for life and true religion" (2 Peter 1:3).

We need to create our own little quiet island or isolated space in our homes at a convenient time each day; preferably the best part of the day which is the early morning time, where we can retreat daily, away from all the clamour of this world, to focus and spend time with Jesus. This enhances our abilities and enables us to hear His voice. "The Lord has given me the tongue of one who has been instructed to console the weary with a timely word; he made my hearing sharp every morning that I might listen like one under instruction. The Lord God opened my ears and I did not disobey or turn back in defiance." (Isaiah 50:4-5).He awakens me every morning and enhances my spiritual hearing, tuning me into the frequencies of His voice and spiritual sounds of the universe.

God loves each one of us dearly, and waits for us to turn to Him. God loves to spend time with us. When we refrain from the pleasures of this world and routinely designate time, specifically for Him; God promises us His unending Joy of the Holy Spirit of God. (Isaiah58:13-14) "You will **find joy in the LORD**, and **I shall make you ride on the heights of the earth**". We as spirit beings cannot serve two masters, i.e. God and Satan; similarly we must not indulge in all the immorality and pleasures of this world, as they are contrary to God's laws.

(Song of Songs 2:10) "My beloved spoke saying to me: '**Rise up, my darling, my fair one come away**". God calls us to separate ourselves from worldly pleasures. Our choices here on earth are extremely important, because God is not someone who will force us to do anything. We are given the opportunity to choose. However there are consequences for the wrong choices. (Proverbs 1:29-33) "Because they detested knowledge and chose not to fear the LORD, because they did not accept my counsel and spurned all my reproof, now they will eat the fruit of their conduct and have a surfeit of their **own devices**; . . . . but **whoever listens to me will live without a care, undisturbed by misfortune**". In our present world of technology, 'man' has designed all sorts of distractions in the form of gadgets, **devices;** and these can be very distracting, and we must never let these distractions control us. Bask in the love of God, trusting Him each day with faith like a child. Acknowledge Him at all times; and He will direct your paths. Even when we are busy, God is always with us, though we may not realise it or we may ignore His presence; He is faithful and will never leave us or forsake us. His love for us is unending.

"I shall win for my people praise and renown throughout the whole world" (Zephaniah 3:19).

"**Ye are a chosen race**, a royal priesthood, a dedicated **nation, a people claimed by God for His own**" (1Peter 2:9).

You are God's very own people who are extremely special to Him.

"YOU . . . . A SPIRITUAL TEMPLE," (1 Peter 2:5).

You are God's special treasure, and He loves every one of His creation.

Chapter 30

Spiritual Emotions

The spirit and physical body of a person is affected by emotions that stem and emerge from within the soul, and result in different human physical actions; depending on the thoughts that we allow in our minds and dwell on. These give shape to the corresponding physical actions. This chain reaction, resulting from an emotion can affect a person's health and well being, either negatively or positively. Every human has the ability, and is capable of being in perfect control of their emotions. Our spirit is the 'silent ruler' over our physical body, since the soul of the spirit person is the seat of all human emotions. When we experience emotions in our spirits, we subconsciously know the answers about how we should react appropriately but we seldom heed our spirits, but go with what the physical body wants to do and overrule our own spirit's opinion. Every human action has a corresponding consequence that is either good or bad.

Some of the greatest people recorded in our Bible faced the harsh consequences for reacting in the wrong physical manner to their momentary heated emotions. There is a lesson that can be learned from the story of Moses, a very well known person recorded in the Bible. Most people are familiar with the miracle story of Moses striking the rock in the desert with his rod and water gushed out of the rock to quench the thirst of the Israelite people. If we carefully read this episode in the Bible we are able to perceive that Moses was not perfect in controlling his emotions, and faced dire consequences as a result.

It must have been terribly hot in the desert that day and the people were tired and thirsty and frustrated due to their long journey in the desert for so many days. Looking back at their past lives and remembering that even though they had been slaves in Egypt at least they had always had water to drink there; made them extremely angry with Moses for bringing them into a desert, where there was no water and living conditions were worse. One can almost visualise the scenario and hear them grumbling and murmuring, some even shouting at Moses, making Moses angry too, because he himself must have been thirsty and feeling the heat of the desert.

God had given Moses and Aaron three clear instructions at this time, and the first one was to **take the rod** the second one was to **gather the people together,** and the third instruction was to **speak to the rock**. God had even reassured Moses that when he spoke to the rock, **it would yield its water**.(Numbers 20:7-8) "The LORD said to Moses, "Take your staff, and then with Aaron your brother assemble the community, and in front of them all command the rock to yield its waters. Thus you will produce water for the community out of the rock for them and their livestock to drink."

But Moses was obviously not thinking or concentrating, he was extremely angry at the people for holding him responsible for their thirst, and he himself was thirsty and feeling the desert heat; so instead of controlling his emotions, he allowed himself to go into a rage. Because he took the rod from the ark as God had instructed him to do, and then he gathered the people and said "Listen, you rebels! Must we get water for you out of this rock" (Numbers 20:10).

This man of faith had completely lost control of his emotions, because he was talking to the people and calling them names ('rebels') and then taking the credit of the miracle for himself for giving them water to drink. One can almost visualise Moses striking the rock in a frenzy of rage, as he struck it twice. When in reality God had told him to speak to the rock, not to the people, and hadn't even told him to strike the rock. So really Moses blundered, in a big way, and the consequences were dire for disobedience and for not taking control of his emotions; and for not believing that God could make the water come out of the rock if he had just spoken to it, thus Moses dishonoured God in the presence of the people.

For his unbelief, for not honouring God, for also taking the praise and credit of the miracle for himself, and not doing what he was told to do, God told Moses that he would not enter the Promised Land. If we continue reading the story in the Bible we know that Moses, and even Aaron (who was along with Moses), eventually died in the desert because of their unbelief. Moses was told later on in the story by God to climb the mountain and die. He could see the 'Promised land' from the top of the mountain, but he was not allowed to enter the Promised Land.

The lesson for us clearly demonstrated in this story is the fact that if we take control of our emotions and channel the very same energy positively into words, by speaking to our problems they will yield to our words and give the desired positive outcome. This can be compared to moving metaphorical mountains and rocks. To do this successfully one has to master the art of controlling one's own emotions, and believing God, which comes with a lot of effort on our part, but is achievable with supernatural help in our spirits from the Holy Spirit of God.

Obedience is also a key into the supernatural world of God which exists all around us, unseen with our physical eyes. Positive emotions that are controlled—set in motion positive thoughts—which bring about positive words—that create positive energy—resulting in positive actions—creating positive things to come out of the supernatural unseen world—and become a reality in our physical world. Positive emotions link good relationships, and similarly good things, also bringing positive reactions. Obedience stems from an emotion that is controlled. It is our choice to control our emotions or to let them spiral out of control.

Any human act of disobedience stems from an emotion that is out of control. Before a negative emotion creates a thought it must be curbed, to ensure that there are no negative actions.

Angry emotions make angry thoughts, angry words and angry sounds which in turn create angry wave patterns in the atmosphere; and similarly angry ripples in our bodies, which consist of so much fluid. These becomes like an angry wave that washes over one's whole being eventually; and affects one's wellbeing physically and spiritually. Any emotion, does all of the above. This is why the Bible specifies "a glad heart makes for good health, but low spirits sap one's strength" (Proverbs 17:22).

Happy emotions are like a medicine to our body bringing about healing and health. Sad emotions or emotions of unforgiveness and hurt make unhappy thoughts, unhappy words and unhappy sounds. These create unhappy electrical circuits and wave patterns, and again similarly unhappy ripple patterns in the human body that is feeling this emotion; which then overwhelms the person, just like a wave of the ocean.

People need to be aware of how important it is to control one's own emotions and not allow the emotion to control you, whether it is a feeling of loneliness, anger, love, hate, unforgiveness, or any other emotion; because the spiritual emotion then transfers to the physical human body, and its lasting effects are visibly seen in the physical body. For example, emotional hurts can manifest in the human physical body and be seen as depression, or pain.

The way to cope with this particular emotion is to replace the hurt and emotional pain **with the joy of the Holy Spirit** and allow God to work on your spirit, in the spirit world, by the supernatural power of God. Let go of emotions of hate and hurt and unforgiveness and anger or loneliness and do not dwell on these thoughts at all; replace them with happy thoughts, because the thoughts that one may dwell on long enough eventually trigger actions.

Thoughts create electrical circuits and waves in the human body, and the unseen world around us. We know this to be true by the fact that medical science can record brain waves of a person even when people are asleep and dreaming; their thoughts are making waves, recordable on a graph called an electro-encephalogram (EEG). Our brain and body cells communicate with each other via electrical impulses.

Very clear instructions are given about things that are **true**, things that are **honest,** things that are **just,** things which are **pure**, things that are **lovely**, and things which have a **good report**, we are told to **meditate on these things**. A process of observing, listening, speaking aloud and ruminating on these things and words that affect our thought pattern is included in the procedure of meditation which can positively change the mathematical calculations and structure of our thought patterns that dominate the human personality. Humans can literally control emotions just by dwelling deliberately on positive thoughts, which in turn affect the person's well-being positively. (Philippians 4:8) "and now, my friends, all that is true, all that is noble, all that is just and pure, all that is lovable and attractive, whatever is excellent and admirable, fill your thoughts with these things".

The instruction to **meditate** indicates the need to set aside time each day, to **think** with utmost concentration and to **read, write** and **speak** aloud about good things. The importance of documentation is that it confirms one's declaration and defines it permanently. When we declare and write down our meditations we are confirming them in the spiritual realm, because anything written down is a job done, confirmed, and it will surely then manifest in the natural or physical world; as it becomes like a legal document. Quoting scripture verses aloud and praising God by singing and even just speaking, enhances the process of changing negative thoughts to positive thoughts.

Anyone can judge a person's mood or feelings by the body language of a person. Whether a person is in pain or depressed or sad or happy or angry; these stem from emotions in the soul, that were felt in the spirit of that person giving rise to thoughts that create words and actions. These then radiated to the surface of their physical human body and manifested in whatever form of emotion they were feeling; enabling the observer to just look and know what emotion was being felt by the person observed.

The effect of the transmission of thoughts, words and actions by the electrical currents that exist in our body, and the phenomenon of waves, makes it possible for emotions to manifest in the flesh. So if a person is in control of their emotions, they decide consciously or subconsciously, what they are going to feel; whether it is love hatred, anger or calmness, sadness or joy. Never let your emotions spiral out of control as the consequences are dire. If for whatever reason they are out of control, we just need to ask God to help us and He very graciously steps in and makes the necessary mathematical corrections in the electrical systems of our body, that realign our emotional settings, to manufacturers settings, bringing healing in the core (soul) of the human spirit that sets everything in perfect order.

If you want to change your life, you need to change your thought pattern, take control of your emotions, and replace harmful thoughts with good thoughts; by deliberately thinking good thoughts and speaking them out aloud, so that beautiful electrical patterns may be set in motion.

When a stone is thrown into a pond, it initially starts a small ripple in the water, which slowly spreads out around it, making a larger ripple and ripples till it reaches the sides of the whole pond. Our thoughts in the same manner create ripples in our physical body till it reaches the surface of the physical body. When an emotion becomes visible in the manifestation of body language that represents the emotion; it does not conclude here; because the unseen electrical circuits are set in motion. This emotion is then transferrable to another human in the form of a word or action, and can also affect the other person's mood or their emotions. For example emotions of anger or love result in similar thoughts and corresponding actions, and can be felt by another person in the room, just by your body language, or the words when you speak to them, or your facial expressions. Emotions—thoughts—words—actions, create powerful unseen circuits that are almost tangible. We often use the expression 'I could have cut the atmosphere with a knife', indicating that a tension in the room was present and could be sensed with our physical senses; even if words or actions were absent. The thought pattern being sent out creates an atmosphere that is 'electric'.

Negative thought patterns that are not corrected eventually have a negative effect on a person's health and well being, and cause stress leading to different health issues; only because the human body is out of synchronisation with the spirit and soul and emotions are allowed to overrule uninterrupted.

Control your emotions, Change your thoughts! Change your words! Change your actions! Change your world! You are in control of your emotions.

When we commit all our ways to God, then our thoughts will be established by God, and we will not have to struggle with unwanted, unclean thoughts. The Lord himself will ensure that our thoughts are appropriate and excellent. (Proverbs 16:3) "Commit to the Lord all that you do, and your plans will be successful".

Thoughts are powerful. Let's create a world where love abounds, by sending out ripples, circuits of positive happy thoughts of love that will turn into words and actions, making each one of us more aware and sensitive to the needs of others around us. Have you ever wondered how the atmosphere around a happy person feels? If you remain in that same atmosphere long enough you would feel happy too.

Don't let your mind function in auto pilot, because it then thinks all sorts of things, and soon spirals out of control, just like a car would if allowed to move without anyone directing its path or controlling its speed. Most people are not even aware of the thinking mechanism of our brains, and that there are modes or settings that can be utilised; or that we can control our thought life all the time. They allow random thoughts to dominate their thinking most of the time, due to being unaware of the fact that they are the final authority on every thought that crosses their minds, and that it is their choice whether to entertain it or discard it.

Our human intuitive mode of thinking can be compared to an auto pilot mode, where quick decision making is familiarly done on a daily basis by every person. Only when faced with difficult decisions, we use analytical thinking with an in-depth reflection on everything that is relevant.

Yet **every thought is connected to an emotion** whether we are aware of it or not, but we allow ourselves to function on auto pilot most of the time because this is how we are wired to do things, and it is easy and simple, but so dangerous. We seriously need to give more thought to our random thoughts, and train ourselves to think in the more analytical mode all the time, ensuring a crop of good fruitful thoughts. "Guard your heart (soul-mind) more than anything you treasure, for it is the source of all life" (Proverbs 4:23); fix your thoughts on Jesus (Hebrews 3:1) "think of Jesus" are the instruction given to us in the Bible, indicating that it is so important to control your thought life to enjoy good mental health.

Thoughts are like seeds which when sown in the soil will germinate and grow and multiply. Anything out of control creates large amounts of vibrations, oscillations that can be measured. Vibrations always make a sound, whether it is in a miniature measurement scale or a large audible scale, they can be heard and felt; and loud noises heard all the time are very tiring and can stimulate our pain sensors. Thoughts out of control create vibrations as their electrical circuits have gone haywire. Don't let your thoughts spiral out of control and then have them silenced with antidepressants, which are just lowering the tone of their vibrations so that they are not audible to you.

Humans try to cope in many different ways with these out of control thoughts and emotions, and some try alcohol or drugs or so many other methods that don't work, as the root cause is never eliminated by these substances or measures. There is a need to cut off these thoughts from the root, by training ourselves to curb every negative thought and casting it out of our minds, so that it never develops or sets in motion any electrical circuits that may cause a vibration or give it a voice.

Our physical bodies and muscles can be toned and shaped and made physically fit and good looking with physical exercise. Similarly our spiritual body can be shaped and toned and strengthened by spiritual exercises, that include meditation on God's 'Word', as it replaces all the negative thoughts with positive thoughts and words; bringing about good spiritual and mental health. Because thoughts exist in the unseen realm and stem from our emotions from the 'brain in the gut', the soul, connected to our spirit man, they still affect our physical realm because of the nano—electrical circuits they create; and therefore need to be exercised and channelled in a specific direction and on a specific pathway. They should not be allowed to metaphorically drive down the motor way out of control without a driver at the steering wheel.

We are instructed to take captive every thought to make it obedient to Christ. Our spirit and our flesh body are constantly battling thoughts that stem from our soul and the emotions that are generated there. This is the point of access in the spirit world where a person can communicate with either the demonic spiritual realm or the spiritual realm of our Creator God. Depending on where we are connected spiritually will define the outcome of our emotions and thoughts being controlled externally or supernaturally, even though we may not be aware of this realm at all.

Demons battle for our souls in the spirit world and can even control our emotions and thought patterns if we allow them to, either legally or in ignorance. If we are not spiritually connected to Jesus, we are open to be targeted by demon spirits. The Bible alerts us, informing us that "our struggle is not against human foes, but against cosmic powers, against the authorities and potentates of this dark age, against the superhuman forces of evil in the heavenly realms."(Ephesians 6:12). Demon spirits exist in the unseen spiritual world around us. We are also told that though we are flesh, we must not war according to the flesh to overcome these problems, but we have been given spiritual weapons which work to keep our minds safe from attack in the spirit realm to protect our soul.

We can take captive every thought to make it obedient to Christ. We can cast down imaginations and every vain thing that exalts itself against the knowledge of God. This can be done by very simply speaking out loud the relevant Bible verses for every circumstance.

Every thought can be controlled. Don't ever dwell on negative thoughts and negative emotions and negative situations, create a positive environment even in the face of negative situations and they will soon turn around the situation to a positive outcome; this can be done just by verbally confessing God's positive words out loud. "Your word is revealed and all is light; it gives understanding even to the untaught" (Psalm 119:130). When God's words enter our soul, and spirit it gives light, the light switch is turned on; which changes the electrical circuits in our thought pattern. "The words I have spoken to you are both spirit and life" (John 6:63); because they make the complicated mathematical calculation changes required for the miniature nano—electrical circuits in our brains and brain waves, that is the control room of our physical body and spiritual bodies; to function perfectly.

There is no dividing line that separates the spirit, soul and body of a human, as they all merge into one another as one; but "The Word of God is alive and active. It cuts more keenly than any two edged sword, piercing so deeply that it divides soul and spirit, joints and marrow; it discriminates among the purposes and thoughts of the heart" (Hebrews 4:12).The words of God are able to discern the thoughts and intents of our hearts, and also have the power to change them if we will confess God's words aloud and meditate on them. This is why anything that we do physically or spiritually, both affect our natural body in corresponding similar aspects.

There is a warning that we can heed, and an instruction that we can apply to practice in our lives, to live victoriously. This warning and instruction had been given to Cain (as recorded in the Bible) before he killed his brother Abel, but Cain did not heed God's instruction or warning at all. We can learn from this experience of Cain, so that we don't make the same mistakes (Genesis 4:6-7) "The LORD said to Cain, 'Why are you angry? Why are you scowling? If you do well, you hold your head up; if not, **sin is a demon crouching at the door; it will desire you and you will be mastered by it**". Cain was upset at the time because his brothers offering had been regarded with favour by the

Lord and his offering was not regarded. His negative emotions turned to negative thoughts and negative actions, because God questioned his reason for anger and his facial expressions of scowling. Cain's negative emotions had surfaced and were physically visible in his body language and facial expressions.

The warning from God to Cain was, and to us still is, that the demon named sin lies at the door of our souls and spirits and literally at the doors of our homes and our lives. This demon spirit named sin is crouching in anticipation.

When someone crouches it indicates that the person is deceitful and crafty, trying to hide while they are lying in wait, ready to pounce on or spring up at any given opportunity. Anyone crouching or lying outside a doorway is usually someone who has a very low social status in life and has no self esteem or scruples at all. We would all be wary of such people if we encountered them. Similarly these demons lie in wait in the spiritual realm, and we are now made aware of them. Anyone in a lying crouching position is usually vulnerable, and can be trampled upon. These demon spirits have no authority in our lives unless we give them any access.

We have complete authority over these demons spirits when we have the Holy spirit of God living on the inside of us. So we must not give these demon spirits access into our spirits, as they will jump in at any given opportunity and take control of the person's life, making them slaves to sin and making them do things that they would never do otherwise. We must not dwell on negative emotions or emotions of anger, because they will then get transported from our soul and spirit to our physical body and manifest as thoughts and negative actions; which if we continue to dwell on, then gives the demon 'sin' a mode of entry and access to a person's soul, spirit and body.

This is exactly what happened to Cain, as depicted in the Bible, because Cain allowed his thoughts of anger and dejection to spiral out of control, as he dwelt on them long enough; and let them ripple through his inner most being, from the soul of his spirit to his flesh mind, or brain, which turned these emotions into physical words and actions of anger. He continued to dwell on these emotions inspite of being reminded by God that he had the authority to rule over these emotions and the demon 'sin'. Cain who did not control his emotions was later controlled by his emotions because the demon spirit 'sin 'gained access to his soul, got into him and caused him to go into a frenzy of rage and these emotions now converted to drastic physical actions, because three physical actions were performed by Cain as described in the Bible (Genesis 4:8) "Cain **said** to his brother Abel, 'let us go out into the country.' Once there, Cain **attacked** and **murdered** his brother."

- **He talked** to his brother 'Abel'; which was most likely in a rage of angry words.
- **He rose up**, or got himself into a position to overpower his brother.
- **He killed** his brother

'Sin' the demon spirit completely controlled Cain and made him to do this, turning him into a murderer. It was not the end of the outcome of his uncontrolled emotions; because Cain then also lied to God when he was questioned about the whereabouts of his brother. 'Sin', now had a body (Cain's body, which he had jumped into, and taken possession of) which he used to lie to God. 'Sin' took full control of Cain's life and completely ruined his future as well, because Cain became a vagabond. **Sin having the reins to** Cain's life, the very core, **his soul; could now generate all** Cain's **emotions** as he pleased making him a complete puppet to sin.

Knowledge about the enemy's strategy should make us alert, and encourage us to quickly get rid of emotions that give place to anger or any other negative thoughts; and immediately replace these emotions and thoughts with positive emotions and thoughts of peace, calm and joy. Speak to the demon named 'sin' and command him to leave, in the authority of the name of Jesus.

Emotions out of control are dangerous (James 1:15) "then desire conceives and gives birth to sin, and sin when it is full-grown breeds death". Any desire that is selfish or has negative thoughts, are emotions out of control or unchecked emotions that have been dwelt on for a long period of time. When we leave emotions to run amok, out of control, it secures a place in our spirit, unseen spiritual electrical circuits are created and set in motion; similar to a human womb. These create favourable conditions to receive the seed of the demon spirit named 'sin'-which in due time is birthed, as one keeps encouraging thoughts and emotions causing desire. When the demon named 'sin' is born in a person's spirit; it grows and becomes full-grown bringing about the death of the person's spirit.

Desires are extremely dangerous emotions and must never be encouraged. These emotions must be nipped in the bud; never dwelt on, and always replaced with other more pleasant powerful thoughts from God's words —the Bible.

There is an emotion and a desire that is healthy for all human spirits and must be encouraged and dwelt upon (Isaiah 26:9) "With all my heart I long for you in the night, at dawn I seek for you". The soul of any human is always yearning for God and has a feeling of emptiness or a hollow feeling, which is a spiritual need to connect with God and tap into the power supply spiritually, because we all are spirit beings. Our soul desires or has this emotion for a communication with God, and during the day all the five physical senses drown out the needs of the spirit and soul. At night when a human is asleep and all five senses are toned down and all is quiet, the soul is able to influence our emotions the most at this time; and yearns for God making the spiritual contact, that makes ripples or circuits to the spirit man who then wakes up early to seek God. The emotion (desire) is the circuit of contact with God, or is the life line that makes the spirit turn these ripples or circuits of emotion in the soul into actions (seeking) in the spirit. It takes a matter of time from night to early morning for the emotion felt in the soul to ripple through the spirit person and convert this emotion into physical action in the early hours of the morning to seek God.

Our soul communicates with God when we are asleep at night. (Song of Songs 5:2) "I sleep but my heart (soul) is awake. Listen! My beloved is knocking . . . open to me my perfect one". Our spirit seeks God early in the morning making the connection in our flesh body. It then becomes our choice whether we allow the physical body to communicate with God or not. When humans cut off the communication line with God by choosing not to commune with God in the physical human body it restricts healing and health only to the spirit and soul and it causes a technical blockage in the flesh physical body causing malfunctions.

"I **offer** you the **choice** of **life or death, blessing or curse. Choose life** and **you** and **your descendents** will **live**; love the Lord your God, obey Him, and hold fast to Him: that is life for you and length of days on the soil which the Lord swore to give to your forefathers, Abraham, Isaac, and Jacob" (Deuteronomy 30:19).

There is a life line, connecting us to God, our source of all life. God refers to this as a silver cord; that connects us to our creator God. This cord is unseen in the spirit realm, and the Bible briefly mentions this contact line with God; that is just like an umbilical cord which connects us to our mother in the womb. When this silver cord is broken, it is then the end of our physical life on the earth in our earth suits or physical bodies. The preacher comments about this: "Remember your creator before the silver cord is snapped" (Ecclesiastes 12:6). At the end of our journey in this life, it is the **spirit** that **returns** to God and the physical body to dust (Ecclesiastes 12:7) "the dust returns to the earth as it began and the spirit returns to God who gave it."

The life of the spirit person does not end here on earth, because there is eternal life beyond the earth suit. The awareness of being a spirit person is not adequate and is incomplete if one does not act upon this information. It is important to get ready, take the Word of God and the oil of the Holy Spirit in our vessels and Go . . . tell the world. We are living in the last days; it is nearing the end of time and we must be ready. For every different stage in life there is particular special oil that the Lord has prepared for each of us. The oil of joy for mourning and the garment of praise for a spirit of heaviness, and the oil of gladness, different oils for different stages and needs in life.

Jesus was transfigured in view of his disciples Peter, James and John, some days before he was crucified. It is important to note that transfiguration involves a change in substance, appearance and form, rendering the change luminous and beautiful. In a similar manner before the return of the Lord Jesus "Those who are wise shall shine as the brightness of the firmament, and those who turn many to righteousness like the stars forever and ever" (Daniel 12:3). There will be divine intervention for the human spirits who trust in Jesus. There will be a transformation and transfiguration of persons.

Chapter 31

Broken Spirits

Our words can cause distress to others or may soothe and comfort others, and bring joy to their lives; depending on the category of words we may choose to use. All words stem from our emotions, and every human has control over their emotions. To control one's emotions is a choice we all have; and whether we choose to use it or not, it is a choice of every individual. Jesus is our healer and is the God who heals us when we go to Him, and ask him to forgive us and heal us. "I create the fruit of the lips Peace, peace to him . . . . I will heal him" (Isaiah 57:19).

There are many different emotions that are the cause of a broken spirit, for example, unforgiveness, sorrow, envy and perverseness; all these are the root cause of health problems that eventually manifest in the physical body of a person. (Proverbs 15:4) "A soothing word is a tree of life, but a mischievous tongue breaks the spirit." Spoken words are actions of our thoughts originating from emotions; and any words that are perverse are not edifying, they are destructive. Spoken words are powerful; they have unseen abilities to construct or destroy. Negative words arising from negative emotions are extremely dangerous weapons. Adultery destroys the soul of a person. "So one who commits adultery is a senseless fool: he dishonours the woman and ruins himself" (Proverbs 6:32).

Emotions of unforgiveness are self destructive. Unforgiveness stems from emotions that have been set in motion due to another person's (or spirit's) words or actions, which may have caused emotional or physical hurt. Harboured unforgiveness can cause a festering in one's soul, and over time becomes a toxic abscess in one's inner most being, that is similar to a time bomb that is ticking and getting ready to explode and destroy anything and everything in its path.

God mentions unforgiveness as a cause for a broken spirit (Proverbs 15:13) "heartache crushes the spirit". Heart ache or sorrow is always caused by something that happens externally. This external factor upsets the soul and gives rise to internal negative emotions that surface as a result. Unforgiveness is one of these negative emotions, which cause a bad feeling. It is evident that sorrow causes a broken spirit; because this festering abscess of unforgiveness induces a malfunction in the electrical power supply, in the human body that affect the circuits, and render the spirit of that person to be broken. This is almost like having a leg or an arm or the neck broken physically, which causes the person to become vulnerable and helpless; the immune system is affected and may break down, affecting the whole person and making the individual more susceptible to disease.

In the human body, or the flesh part of a human, when an abscess is allowed to exist without being treated either medically or surgically, it soon affects the whole body, even though it may be locally contained inside tissue of a specified isolated area. Any physical abscess will soon cause a malfunction physically, raising the body temperature and causing physical pain. It may also present many different signs and symptoms in the body, for example: inflamed localised skin, or a raised body temperature causing rigors that affect the whole body. This can go on and cause havoc in the body until the abscess is treated either medically or surgically.

Emotions of unforgiveness do exactly the same thing, and can be compared similarly as it causes a spiritual abscess, which initially may be localised, but eventually will radiate to the whole body; just like ripples in a pond of water that is disturbed. It then manifests in the flesh body in the form of a disease, because it is the cause of unease (Proverbs 17:22)"low spirits sap one's strength". A spirit that is broken is responsible for ill health of the bones, causing it to dry; according to the Bible. "If you forgive others the wrongs they have done, your heavenly Father will also forgive you; but if you do not forgive others, then your Father will not forgive the wrongs that you have done" (Matthew 6:14).

The need to forgive people who have hurt us is so important, in order to enjoy good health yourself. By forgiving the other person you are actually doing yourself a favour, because God can then work in your life to bring about the desired healing; whereas if you do not forgive others or even yourself, you unknowingly create a wall in the spiritual realm between you and God, that blocks out your own blessings of healing and health. It is only you who can knock down the wall of unforgiveness, to be able to receive from God.

By studying human biology we are made aware that bones manufacture all the red blood cells in our body that pertain to life. When this malfunctions the effect is disastrous. Treating the symptoms that manifest as a disease, but being unable to treat the cause, due to being oblivious of the spirit person that lives in the human body, results in a recession of the disease; until the next lot of symptoms surface like a ripple from the soul. An abscess usually requires surgical intervention to drain the pus or diseased tissue, and can be extremely painful when incised. Similarly spiritual abscesses caused by unforgiveness may be painful when being treated by our creator God, and may cause us some amount of spiritual and physical discomfort.

But there is hope yet, which includes individual choices. To treat unforgiveness in order to mend a broken spirit, one has to deal with the emotions of unforgiveness and get rid of it, by changing these emotions to forgiveness. The only possible manner in which this can be done is by allowing the love of God to flow through us to the people who have hurt us (Romans 5:5) "Such hope is no fantasy; through the Holy Spirit he has given us, God's love has flooded our hearts". Like a river, this love uproots unforgiveness and clears it out, dredging our soul of all these negative toxic emotions that had been allowed to settle there.

God's love floods our hearts causing love to overflow to others (just like flood waters overflow) and also washing out all the impurities of the soul. Flowing water that is pure, fresh and clean tastes good; unlike stagnant water that is stale, has impurities and tastes awful. Unseen electrical circuits that connect our spirit, soul and body get restored when we choose and allow God to intervene and assist us with his river of love, and when we forgive willingly and intentionally all the people in our lives who have caused us hurt. When we renew our minds with the Word of God we are able to lift our heads up and open the gates to our hearts to let the King of glory in.(Psalm 24:9-10) "Lift up your heads, you gates, lift them up you everlasting doors, that the King of Glory may come in. Who is this King of Glory? The LORD of HOSTS, He is the king of glory."We all need God's assistance to restore and renew everything, without Him this cannot be achieved.

One has to choose to speak aloud words of forgiveness to those who have hurt you (not necessarily directly to the person concerned); to enable the process of restoring electrical circuits in our bodies, to manufacturer's settings and be healed. When we perform these actions we facilitate the process of clearance where all blockages that are clogging our systems are removed. The direct line of communication is restored with our Creator, and the conveyor belt of our blessings is set in motion again as the walls come crumbling down in the spiritual realm; that were built up due to unforgiveness and were stopping the flow of the blessings from God.

As we convert and replace these negative emotions with positive emotions, they initiate and stimulate positive thoughts, which trigger positive actions which ripple through the circuits of the human body causing happy ripples and restoring good health, which continues to ripple in the atmosphere like waves affecting others around you, causing healing to their emotions too as you forgive them. Happiness always rubs off onto others, too (Proverbs 17:22) "A glad heart makes for good health".

Broken spirits require mending, and there are many broken spirits in our world today. So let's deliberately start ripples of healing that will eventually move out and touch the lives of others around us in a positive aspect.

The Law of God is a fountain, Spirit of Wisdom is a flowing brook of life, Spirit of Council is deep waters, Spirit of the fear of the Lord is instruction, and the Spirit of Understanding is a wellspring of life; flowing from God to our souls.

Instruction is from the Father (heavenly-Holy Spirit-'He') and Law is from the Mother (heavenly-Wisdom-'She'). Proverbs 1:8 "Attend my son to your **Father's instruction** and do not reject your **mother's teaching"**. We must acknowledge our earthly and heavenly parents, following instructions and keeping their commands obediently. We have instructions and laws set out for us in the book of Proverbs in the Bible; that give us clear directions for our life.

The grace and favour of God be with you all. May *"You a spiritual being"* enable all who read it to experience the presence of Jesus, gain an insight to enhance your spiritual lives and make the right choices; by delving into the Bible and finding more spiritual nuggets for a victorious Christian life.

01864-86784920-1082-2486-6001-760804-3216-71113 5683
1080.005-750-M (squared) 076>17 417345-803-1133-141178-7842-
269-1001 - 13 cm by 10 cm.